Easy Mini-Lessons for Building Vocabulary

◀◀◀◀◀◀◀◀◀◀◀◀◀◀◀◀◀◀◀◀◀◀◀◀◀◀◀◀◀ ▶▶▶▶▶▶▶▶▶▶▶▶▶▶▶▶▶▶▶▶▶▶▶▶▶▶▶▶▶

Practical Strategies That Boost Word Knowledge and Reading Comprehension

By Laura Robb

SCHOLASTIC
PROFESSIONAL BOOKS

NEW YORK ● TORONTO ● LONDON ● AUCKLAND ● SYDNEY
MEXICO CITY ● NEW DELHI ● HONG KONG

for my daughter, Anina,

poet and teacher,

who loves language and words.

Front cover and interior design by Kathy Massaro
Cover and interior photographs by Bonnie Forstrum Jacobs

ISBN 0-590-26466-4

Contents

Acknowledgments

When Terry Cooper, editor-in-chief of Scholastic Professional Books, asked me to consider writing a book for teachers about vocabulary, I immediately accepted. I thank Terry for this suggestion, one that has caused me to reflect about vocabulary instruction and how young and old learn words.

My deepest thanks to Wendy Murray, my editor, who suggested I add mini-lessons to the book so teachers would have clear models to guide them. Wendy's terrific insights have helped me shape and organize this book.

To Heather Campbell and Steve Clegg, fourth- and fifth-grade teachers at Quarles Elementary School in Winchester, Virginia, my sincere appreciation for including many of these strategies in your teaching day and sharing students' work with me. Thanks also to Gretchen Saunders, sixth-grade teacher at Daniel Morgan Middle School.

How appreciative I am of the trust and support of John Lathrop, head of Powhatan School in Boyce, Virginia, who has encouraged me to continue writing about teaching. Thanks also to Diane Carpenter and Nancy Lee, principals in the Winchester City Public Schools, who have encouraged me to work with their teachers.

My work with struggling readers has helped me to recognize that in conjunction with improving students' reading rate, fluency, and comprehension, I had to develop their appetite for learning new words. Just as nourishing foods improve health, a rich and varied vocabulary improves reading. My students remind me of the relationship between a strong vocabulary and proficient reading every time one of them says, "I can't read this; It's too hard. I don't know enough words." And so to my students, sincere thanks for teaching me well. Your willingness to try strategies and your honesty in evaluating each one have enabled me to fine-tune all of the ideas in this book.

Most important, I thank my husband, Lloyd, who spent hours reading early drafts and critiquing them. His enthusiastic support and ongoing encouragement have enabled me to write this book.

Introduction

More than 30 years ago, I stepped into my first classroom crowded with 34 boys and girls. My teaching supplies consisted of a sixth-grade basal reader plus social studies and science textbooks. These were for teaching a range of readers from struggling to on-grade to proficient. Of course, more than half the class could not read the books, but that was all I had. As several students put it, "We don't have enough words to understand what those books mean." Even though many of these weak readers could pronounce the words in each text, they did not understand what the words meant. What's more, as the year unfolded, I discovered that they lacked strategies for figuring out the meanings of words that stumped them. At that point in my career I was a novice, without the experience and

Seventh grader Jaime compares her context definition of a word with the dictionary's definition.

knowledge to provide students with useful strategies. Even more frustrating was the way the teaching guides for these textbooks structured vocabulary lessons.

The lessons invariably instructed teachers to copy a list of key words and definitions onto the chalkboard before reading a book or studying a topic. I'd dutifully read the list aloud to students—sometimes as many as 10 to 15 words, especially in science and geography. Halfway through this recital, I'd look up to discover that most students were engaged in "learning avoidance" activities, such as staring out the window, passing notes, yawning, or resting their heads on desks! Determined to succeed, I would encourage students to copy the word lists into notebooks, but this didn't improve their interest in or recall of these new words.

Discouraged, I asked my students, "Why don't you listen to the vocabulary introductions? Why don't you recall the words after you study them?" Here are some of the students' replies, which I saved from that first year. In italics is what students' words mean to me now. Their words are nuggets of wisdom that have greatly influenced my vocabulary instruction today:

☀ They [the words] don't stick in my head.

For readers to start to understand new words, connections between the unfamiliar word and the learner's experience must be forged.

☀ It's boring.

Information, such as new words, that has no meaning to learners is irrelevant and uninteresting.

☀ It's hard to pay attention after the third word.

Learners remain engaged in a task when the activity has relevance to their experiences and knowledge. Moreover, introducing more than four to five new words can overwhelm and frustrate students.

☀ I can figure some [words] out when I read. But I don't always remember what they mean outside of the reading.

Context clues help readers understand new words. For recall of new words to occur from context, learners must repeatedly meet words in their reading.

It has taken me years of classroom experience as well as reading professional books and journals to translate these students' comments into effective vocabulary strategies.

A primary purpose for this book is to place these valuable tools into many teachers' hands. With television, videos, and computers, the students you and I teach read less than students of previous generations, and their word knowledge suffers. As we guide students to become lifelong, independent readers, nudging them along with wonderful novels and read-alouds, we must not forget to provide the vocabulary instruction necessary to improve students' word knowledge.

Not too long ago, I interviewed 90 fifth and sixth graders who read two to three years below grade level. My questions probed three issues:

1. Can you pinpoint when you started to dislike reading?

2. Can you tell me what's easy for you while reading? What's hard?

3. How can your teachers help you improve?

The second fifth grader I interviewed cut right to the heart of the matter: "Give me words so I can read the books and give me books that I can read."

Most reading problems that we identify as comprehension problems usually relate to vocabulary deficiencies. If the meanings of just a few key words in a passage are unknown, then there is little to no comprehension. As you read this book, you'll discover mini-lessons, vocabulary-building strategies, and word-study activities that are designed to decrease vocabulary deficiencies. They can and should be integrated into subjects across the curriculum. Words are one of the most useful learning tools we can offer children. With words we think, read, write, talk, feel, and dream. Whether we use words to express feelings; talk to a friend; or read a magazine, road sign, novel, or poetry, they help us sift through and define our experiences.

Guiding Principles of Vocabulary Instruction

> " Give me words
> so I can read
> the books,
> and give me books
> I can read. "
>
> —*Fifth Grader*

Fourth graders discuss their synonym and antonym lists.

erb is a fifth grader who devours books. On his desk is a stack of paperbacks. "I can't wait to start *The Awesome Egyptians*," he tells me. Besides in-line skating, Herb's "favorite thing in all the world to do is read." All teachers want a room filled with Herbs. His appetite for reading guarantees that he continuously gains proficiency and learns new words. By repeatedly meeting unfamiliar words in different contexts, Herb is able to use past experiences with these words, as well as his knowledge of roots, prefixes, and suffixes, to figure out many meanings. Like Herb, children who read, read, and read some more improve and develop their vocabulary and easily advance to higher-level books.

Cassie, a struggling reader, is Herb's classmate. Reading, according to Cassie, is "a boring thing you have to do for school." Two years below grade level, Cassie will continue to fall behind because she reads little. "Why should I read when it takes so long and I don't know what the words mean?" she has said to me. Cassie has nailed her problem: She's a slow, nonfluent reader with a weak vocabulary. Why would she choose to do something that poses so many hurdles?

Cassie and Herb bring to mind a question teachers wrestle with year after year: In the same classroom, how can I find the time to challenge and stimulate the Herbs and also provide the Cassies with strategies that will boost their reading vocabulary? One key to reading success for all students is to provide them with books at their independent level and to teach them with instructional-level books. Sometimes you'll organize students into groups, with each group reading a different title. For several weeks, during reading workshop, you might invite students to select books that interest them. There will be times when you'll want everyone reading the same title—and that's okay. One word of caution, though—it's important that the book selected for whole-class study captivates strong readers while remaining accessible to *all* of your students. To challenge proficient readers and move struggling readers forward during novel studies, make sure all students read additional titles at their independent reading levels.

For proficient and weak readers alike, learning new words takes time and requires that students revisit words again and again. In fact, learning new words to the point that we include them in our writing and daily conversations won't occur in one or two lessons.

Comprehending new words is like dating: You're introduced, take several months to get acquainted, and finally reach a point where you know each other. Unfortunately, teachers have been misguided by teaching guides that imply learning new words occurs rapidly, within two lessons.

Children learn to enjoy words and, in turn, reading when we help them reach a comfort level with new vocabulary. Achieving that comfort level starts when we help students connect an unfamiliar word with past experiences.

The Link to Standardized Test–Taking Skills

Once students love exploring words' meanings, they are on the road to becoming readers, writers, thinkers—and more skilled standardized test takers. Nicole, an eighth grader, in a portfolio entry, noted: "This year I've improved my vocabulary. I can't believe I'm writing this, but I actually enjoy thinking about words. Words help my reading and writing. They help me when we talk about books. My scores on the SSAT (Secondary School Admission Tests) improved in reading and vocabulary because I have become curious about words."

Beyond helping students develop an affection for words, you can prepare

My Progress In Reading

April 15, 1998

Jennifer

    I feel that I have improved a little bit in reading. I feel I am understanding more words in the books I read then before, because of the vocabulary exercises we have been doing. Studying the Latin and Greek roots of words, expands my knowledge of the defanition and helps me understand the word better. Also, learning how most sentences will give you the defanition of a word in a tricky way has helped me. I have learned more defanitions of words and understand them better this year from my reading. Also, I think I am reading a little faster. I think that is a result of reading more books and understanding them better, because of vocabulary. This year I have also been introduced to more books because of the reading contracts.

    I now have a better understanding of what types of books I like to read. When I find books that I like to read, I have discovered that I can concentrate easier on them, and come away remembering most of what I have read. I think that is another one of my

reading improvements. I used to not be able to remember anything I read, but now I can remember almost everything I read. The only thing I have trouble remembering is small details, but I feel I will be able to improve on that also if I keep reading.

An eighth grader, in her evaluation of reading progress, points out how studying Latin and Greek roots improved her vocabulary.

them for standardized tests by familiarizing them with the three kinds of vocabulary questions they'll face: 1. analogies (see page 74); 2. using clues in a sentence or short paragraph to figure out a word's meaning (see page 53); and 3. a word plus four definitions to choose from (see page 35). In addition, cloze reading passages also test students' word knowledge and their ability to use context clues to choose the best word or phrase to fill in the blank.

The strategies and activities in this book can help students deal with these three types of test questions. As you read, look for sidebars throughout called "Standardized Test Link." These contain tips for raising students' awareness of how a strategy can improve test-taking skills.

Teach Vocabulary Before, During, and After Reading

Refining the meaning of a new word will occur as students share experiences, read texts with the word, hear the teacher use the word, and observe how the word functions in sentences. In the classroom, this means teaching vocabulary before, during, and after reading. With this in mind, I've organized the next three chapters around these three stages of reading. You'll find many mini-lessons and vocabulary-building strategies that will enlarge students' word knowledge. Here, then, is an overview of what you'll learn in greater detail as you read later chapters.

Before Reading

Most of us have experienced the meaning of an unfamiliar word—it's just that we're befuddled when confronted with the new word itself. Forging connections between what students already know and the new information they're confronted with is the foundation of vocabulary building. For example, eighth graders have experienced a bad error or poor decision, but few might comprehend the word *egregious*. When teachers introduce new words, they must be careful to think of similar words students already know and build lessons that link the unfamiliar word to students' prior knowledge.

The teacher can select two to five words that students need in order to understand the concepts they'll meet while reading a novel or a science, history, or math chapter. Students can identify unfamiliar words by browsing through a new chapter or multiple titles that relate to a themed study such as oceanography or the industrial revolution.

Here is how science teacher Ray Legge of Powhatan School put this strategy in action: Before charging headlong into a unit on the solar system, Ray wanted to discover which words were unfamiliar to his seventh graders. He organized students into groups of four and displayed sets of books about the solar system on tables. For about 15 minutes, groups of students browsed through books on their tables. While browsing, students jotted down new words in their journals. Mr. Legge recorded this vocabulary on large chart paper. During the four-week unit, students returned to the list of words to refine meanings as their understanding of these terms developed. The list that follows illustrates the words these seventh graders studied intensively:

Chart of Words on Solar System

☀ satellite	☀ asteroid belt	☀ shooting stars
☀ meteoroids	☀ troposphere	☀ speed of light
☀ light years	☀ asteroids	☀ greenhouse effect

During Reading

What's the name of the game for this phase of vocabulary work? *Self-sufficiency.* Providing students with self-help strategies to figure out unfamiliar words gives them the tools to tackle challenging texts with more confidence and determination. A strategy such as segmenting a multisyllable word helps students pronounce new words. Sixth graders Brian and Jack were pair-reading Peg Kehret's *Earthquake Terror.* Brian first pronounced *meandering* as "*mmmming.*" Jack urged him to revisit the word and break it into segments. Brian quickly said, "*me-and-er-ing.*"

Teaching students to spot clues that writers embed in texts is another powerful self-help strategy. Clues that signal that an explanation of a term is nearby encourage students to sleuth out a word's meaning. During a vocabulary discussion, fourth grader Rosa spotlighted how she figured out the meaning of the word *pungent* on page 16 of Jean Craighead George's *The Moon of the Mountain Lion* (HarperCollins). First, Rosa wrote the sentence from the book on the blackboard:

The lion could smell the pungent *cedars the herds were trampling lower down the mountain.* Then Rosa thought out loud: "First, I read the sentence. I could say *pungent*—but I didn't know what it meant. So I looked for clues. It's something the lion smelled—and *pungent* is in front of *cedar*—and that's a tree. So it must be the way cedar trees smell."

Inviting students to share the ways they apply self-help strategies to unlock the meanings of new words provides terrific models for their peers.

After Reading

Between chapters and beyond the novel's end, continue to offer students opportunities to play with words. Explore word origins, other meanings, and their sound effects through webbing, mapping, and word hunts.

Webs invite students to find words related to a core word. The web of words branches out from the center of the page. Webs can focus on synonyms and/or antonyms. Two sixth graders divided a paper in half and created a web with synonyms on the left side and antonyms on the right.

Maps are diagrams that allow students to categorize words and see how word clusters relate to one another. A group of three fifth graders created a map that revealed how much they had learned about bats.

With word hunts, students use reading books to search for synonyms or antonyms. Allison and Kate, fourth graders, skimmed pages in their free-choice reading books and found these synonyms for astonished: *amazed, marveled, astounded,* and *surprised.*

A sixth grader's synonym and antonym web

Such lessons have a double impact: They demonstrate the multiple meanings of words and also raise students' awareness of the importance of word choice in writing.

Using new words, exchanging ideas, and reflection after reading all contribute to a continually deepening understanding of how a word works in

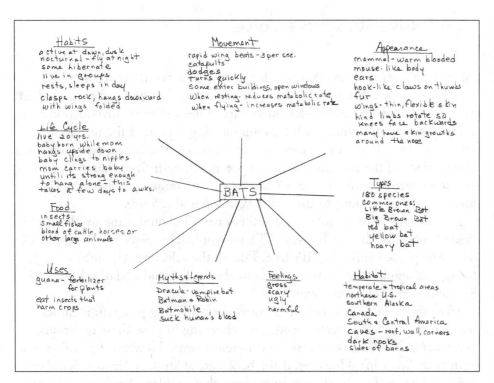

Habits
active at dawn, dusk
nocturnal - fly at night
some hibernate
live in groups
rests, sleeps in day
clasps rock, hangs downward
with wings folded

Movement
rapid wing beats - 3 per sec.
catapults
dodges
turns quickly
some enter buildings, open windows
when resting - reduces metabolic rate
when flying - increases metabolic rate

Appearance
mammal - warm blooded
mouse-like body
ears
hook-like claws on thumbs
fur
wings - thin, flexible skin
hind limbs rotate so
knees face backwards
many have skin growths
around the nose

Life Cycle
live 20 yrs.
baby born while mom
hangs down
baby clings to nipples
mom carries baby
until its strong enough
to hang alone - this
takes a few days to 2 wks.

Food
insects
small fishes
blood of cattle, horses or
other large animals

Types
180 species
common ones:
Little Brown Bat
Big Brown Bat
red bat
yellow bat
hoary bat

BATS

Uses
guana - fertilizer
for plants

eat insects that
harm crops

Myths & Legends
Dracula - vampire bat
Batman & Robin
Batmobile
suck human's blood

Feelings
gross
scary
ugly
harmful

Habitat
temperate & tropical areas
northern U.S.
southern Alaska
Canada
South & Central America
caves - roof, wall, corners
dark nooks
sides of barns

 Fifth graders organize wht they've learned about bats.

our language. Armed with additional knowledge about a word's meaning and how it functions, students can more easily integrate the word into their reading, writing, thinking, and speaking vocabularies.

On pages 16–18 of this chapter, you'll find more activities for building vocabulary.

Key Teaching Principles of a Rich Vocabulary Program

1 Make Explicit Vocabulary Instruction a Three-Times-a-Week Tradition

Use direct instruction and follow-up student practice sessions to equip students with these strategies—effectively using context clues or learning the meanings of word roots, prefixes, and suffixes—that can turn them into word detectives. To accomplish this, you must set aside 10 to 15 minutes, two to three times a week, for students to discuss words with the entire class, a reading partner, or a study group. Exploring the meanings of words is also a worthy activity during unstructured reading-and-writing workshop time.

 Give Students a Voice

"When do *I* get to pick the words for learning?" a fourth grader timidly asked her teacher. My heart fell, for the child's teacher had just presented an exceptional vocabulary mini-lesson as part of her students' introduction to a study of the moon. During a follow-up meeting, I praised the teacher for taking the time to discover students' experiences at the beach, especially their observations of the rise and fall of the ocean. Through their shared stories and some terrific student-drawn blackboard illustrations, most of the class made some connections to the terms *flood tide* and *ebb tide*.

As I rose to leave, wondering whether or not I should bring up the fourth grader's remarks, the teacher said, "Those words have played in my mind all day." She paused and said, "It's true. I do all the selecting. Up until today, I thought I knew which words to choose for study. Maybe I need to let the children pick some words too."

How right she was! A balanced vocabulary-building program includes teacher-*and* student-selected words. Teachers might pose these questions: But what if 24 students each select different words? How can I possibly deal with that? You can't. However, if the books are at students' instructional or independent reading levels, you won't have that problem, because students will be able to read and understand most of the words.

Present Vocabulary Mini-Lessons

Mini-lessons, a practice developed by educators Nancie Atwell and Lucy Calkins, are the ideal teaching technique for showing students how *you* figure out the meaning of new words. Here's an overview of how to conduct them; more detailed examples are sprinkled throughout the book.

During these brief, 10- to 15-minute sessions, first think aloud so students can hear how your mind solves problems as you work to learn unfamiliar words.

Once you've adequately demonstrated a strategy, invite students to complete the demonstration with your support. These collaborations offer struggling or confused learners an opportunity to see how their classmates use the strategy. Observe students during collaborations. If you sense they require more group practice, then provide it. Taking time for working together will enable students to deepen their understanding of how a strategy works and to better apply that strategy in a group or independently.

I encourage students to jot down questions they have as they watch and listen to this process. These questions fuel the follow-up discussion, which is the power behind mini-lessons. The questions students raise and the insights they share provide you with vital information about their level of understanding and/or confusion.

Based on follow-up feedback, you can decide whether or not you should repeat the mini-lesson for the class or a small group, or invite students to dig in and practice the strategy.

▲ *Laura Robb completes a vocabulary quilting chart with students' suggestions (see pages 62–64).*

After the Mini-Lesson, What Next?

The mini-lesson effectively introduces students to a strategy, but unless you provide students with many opportunities to practice that strategy, it will not become a problem-solving tool. My goal is for students to independently apply strategies to their daily reading, to the point where the strategies become second nature. To achieve this goal, I set aside time for students to practice a strategy such as using context clues, or predicting a word's meaning from a knowledge of roots, prefixes, and suffixes, many times during reading workshop. I circulate, observing pairs or groups and note the names of students who have difficulty. As I make the rounds, I pause to answer a question or help move a group along. For those students who "don't get it" after two to three practice sessions, I will model the strategy again with another mini-lesson.

Introduce Vocabulary-Building Activities

Enlarge students' word knowledge with activities that inspire their desire to study our language.

Study Word Parts

Transform your students into word detectives by inviting them to study word origins. (See appendix for a list of roots and origins and eponyms.)

Introduce students to roots (also called derivatives), prefixes, and suffixes, parts of words in our language that come from another language such as Latin, Greek, and Old French. Encourage them to use derivatives to build dozens of words that relate to topics in math, history, geography, science, and English. Seventh graders in prealgebra collected the word list that follows based on the Latin root *equi: equal, equidistant, equivalent, equivalence, equality, equal mark, equilateral, equity, equitable, equitangential, equate, equalization, equilibrium.* When content-area teachers support language arts teachers by incorporating word study into their lessons, students can enlarge their vocabulary.

Hone Vocabulary With Homophones and Homographs

Study *homophones*—words that sound alike, but are spelled differently and have different meanings, such as *weal, wheel, we'll.* (See page 84 for a list of homophones.)

Explore *homographs*—words that are spelled alike, such as *conduct (v.)* and *conduct (n.)*, but whose meanings and parts of speech change as the accented syllable changes—or as the vowel changes from long to short in one-syllable words such as *read* and *read.* (See page 85 for a list of homographs).

Have Fun With Idioms

To fully understand any language, it's necessary to know the language's idioms. If you try to figure out an idiom's meaning word by word, you'll end up perplexed. You have to know what the entire phrase means. "It's raining cats and dogs" in this country means it's really pouring. Outside of our culture people might take these words to literally mean cats and dogs are falling from the sky! To show how much fun you can have with idioms, I've included some of my students' favorites here.

Idiom	Meaning
Ants in Your Pants	restlessness
Behind the Eight Ball	in lots of trouble
Cold Turkey	suddenly stopping a habit
Let the Cat Out of the Bag	gave a secret away
Nothing to Sneeze At	to be taken seriously

Once students understand idioms, have them use one in a sentence. Students often enjoy writing sentences that use an idiom incorrectly, then trading sentences with classmates and replacing the idiom with the correct expression.

Wow Them With Word Histories

Investigate the history of words, and learn how words originated and why their meanings changed. Investigate *eponyms*, words that originate from the names of people. Students will discover fascinating facts about the origins of words, such as the eponym *graham cracker*, named for Dr. Sylvester Graham. (See page 94, for a list of eponyms.)

Invite students to explore *portmanteau*, or blended words, such as *flare*, a blend of *flame* and *glare*. (See Chapter 4 for lists of fun portmanteau words.)

Each week, ask a student to present to the class the history of a word that intrigues or interests him or her.

Word Study Resources

Introduce your students to these books, and you might just spark a romance with words.

Graham-Barber, Lynda. *A Chartreuse Leotard in a Magenta Limousine: And Other Words Named After People and Place*, illustrated by Barbara Lehman. New York: Hyperion, 1994.

Heimlich, Joan E. and Susan D. Pittleman. *Semantic Mapping: Classroom Applications*. Newark, DE: IRA Reading Aids Series, 1990.

Levitt Paul, Douglas Burger, and Elissa Guralnick. *The Weighty Word Book*, illustrated by Janet Stevens. Bouldor CO: Manuscripts, Ltd, 1990.

Terban, Marvin. *Guppies in Tuxedos: Funny Eponyms*, illustrated by Giulio Maestro. New York: Clarion Books, 1988.

Terban, Marvin. *Scholastic Dictionary of Idioms*. New York: Scholastic, 1996.

Urdang, Laurence. *The Basic Book of Synonyms and Antonyms*. New York: Signet, 1978.

The Dictionary: Timing Is Everything

In English, the same word can have multiple meanings. That's why context—how a writer uses a word—can initially help readers struggling with an unfamiliar word more than the dictionary can. For example, take the word *cloud*. *Webster's New Universal Unabridged Dictionary* lists seven definitions for the noun and five for the verb. A fifth grader was asked to use the dictionary to find the definition of *cloud* in this sentence: *She clouded the white yarn with specks of red and purple.* The student wrote, "a visible mass of vapor." Like many other students in his class, he never considered the part of speech and copied the first definition listed, happy to have defined the first word on his list.

Several other students, however, weren't so quick to defer to the dictionary and fared better. They predicted that *clouded* in this sentence meant *dotted* and then searched the dictionary for a meaning similar to their guess. Only when students have read or heard a word used in a sentence and taken time to predict its meaning does the dictionary serve them well. Without some prior knowledge, students cannot choose the right definitions. They often mindlessly copy the dictionary's wording as well as definitions that have nothing to do with the way an author uses the word.

Glossaries: Use Them, but Don't Abuse Them

Glossaries are great clarifiers of a term's meaning, but like the dictionary, students shouldn't flip to them before wrestling with the word on their own. Many teachers send students to the glossary to look up the meanings of new vocabulary words before reading assigned pages in a science, mathematics, or history textbook. However, in my experience, too many students look up the words in the glossary and never complete the reading. "I'll get the general ideas from discussion," an eighth grader told me. "We're only tested on the vocabulary, so why bother to read?" Use the glossary to refine new understandings after students read and discuss a section.

▲ *Eighth graders look up a word to discover its many shades of meaning.*

Closing Reflections

ight guidelines inform my vocabulary instruction. As you read this book and explore specific strategies to weave into your instructional plans, periodically reread these tenets. I do. They refresh my teaching memory, keep me on the right track, and encourage me to constantly evaluate how students and I enlarge our knowledge of words.

GUIDELINES FOR EFFECTIVE VOCABULARY INSTRUCTION

1. READ! READ! AND READ MORE!: The surest way to expand students' vocabularies is by having them read books at their *comfort level*, or independent reading level. No amount of vocabulary instruction can substitute for meeting words, again and again, in different contexts, because repetition helps readers figure out and remember meanings. And read aloud to students every day—this introduces children to new words and word usage in a pleasurable way.

2. AVOID NEW WORD OVERLOAD: Presenting more than two to four new words each week in a subject creates frustration and anxiety, or "new word overload," which results in students having little long-term recall. Eighth graders described their weekly vocabulary test of 10 words—based on a list of 50 new words—as vocabulary roulette. "I never bother to study," said one student. "Why waste time looking up all those words? I take my chances each week. Sometimes I pass, other times I fail."

3. ALLOW STUDENTS TO CHOOSE WORDS TOO: It's appropriate for you and your students to select words for study. By incorporating strategies that invite students to select words they struggle with, you give them the ownership that encourages learning. A fourth grader, reading on a second-grade level, expressed the benefits of ownership when she said, "If I get to pick [words], they're what I don't know. When my teacher does it, she doesn't always get the ones [words] I need."

4. RESERVE CLASS TIME FOR VOCABULARY BUILDING: Since comprehension of texts hinges on word knowledge, then studying vocabulary should be a high priority in your class. During reading/writing workshop, present a weekly vocabulary mini-lesson that models a word-building strategy.

5. CREATIVELY LINK WORDS TO STUDENTS' EXPERIENCE: Find that small nugget of experience or information students have about an unfamiliar word. Then forge the connection, so students can link what they already know to the unfamiliar term. When introducing a word such as *somnambulist*, ask students to brainstorm what they know about *sleepwalking*, a familiar compound word.

6. POINT OUT THE CLUES WRITERS LEAVE: Transform kids into word sleuths. Teach them the words and phrases authors use that signal to the reader that an explanation is lurking nearby. (See page 53 for a complete list of these techniques.)

7. SLOW DOWN, NEW WORD PASSING THROUGH: Words in the English language often have multiple meanings. For example, depending on the way it's used, the noun *hawk*, can mean: a bird of prey; a cheater; an advocate of war; making the sound of forcing phlegm up from the throat. It takes time to absorb the nuances of new words. Repeatedly use them in reading, writing, speaking, and thinking, so students can absorb variations in meaning.

8. EXCHANGE EXPERIENCES WITH WORDS: Set aside time for students to discuss the ways new words connect to their lives. Let them tell one another stories about these words. For example, fourth graders trading stories about the word *astonish* told how a surprise birthday party, a visit from an uncle who lived in Alaska, and a three-foot-high snowstorm all astonished them.

Teach Vocabulary Before Reading or Studying a Topic

> **"Thinking about new words before reading the science chapter made the reading go easier."**
>
> —*Eighth Grader*

Eighth grader Nicole reviews a list of words based on the Latin root, terra.

Early in my career, a fifth-grade class forced me to rethink the way I presented vocabulary. Up until that point, I resisted preteaching any words, believing that this strategy would bore students and create negative attitudes toward a book or a topic. Instead of preteaching, students and I worked on vocabulary as we read and researched. But during a study of simple machines, I knew it was time for a change!

The unit was a tough one, packed with words that I had not studied since my middle school days. Terms such as *fulcrum, lever, effort, pulley,* and *wedge* challenged me. If *I* had to reread passages in the textbook to grasp these concepts, how would my students cope? Obviously, sending them headlong into the study without vocabulary preparation could derail the entire unit. If understanding these principles turned into a monumental struggle, I wondered if these fifth graders would enjoy the unit's creative activity: designing their own simple machines based on the principles we were studying. I developed a vocabulary strategy that contains three steps: 1. Identify the concepts that students need in order to comprehend the reading. 2. Choose three to five words that introduce students to the new concepts. 3. Teach these words in advance of reading and increase students' comprehension. The mini-lesson that follows shows how I put this strategy into effect.

Preteaching Key Concept Words

PURPOSE
to familiarize students with difficult concepts and words before reading

MATERIALS
two to four preselected words, chart paper, markers

SUGGESTIONS FOR PRESENTING YOUR DEMONSTRATION:

1 Identify the key concepts in the passage. This helps you to select the vocabulary words that will boost comprehension.

2 As you select words for preteaching, ask yourself questions such as: Is this word necessary for students to comprehend the passage? Is this word crucial to understanding the main ideas? Which words have clear explanations embedded in the text? Which words are explained through diagrams and illustrations?

3 Eliminate words that you believe students can figure out while reading.

4 Preteach only *two to four words*—more than that will confuse and bore students, especially when they're navigating through totally unfamiliar word and concept territory.

5 Write the words on chart paper. Draw pictures, if that is helpful, that clarify a word's meaning.

6 Connect the new words to meanings that students are familiar with. Forging these connections builds a bridge between what students already know and the new words. For example, to help students understand *perplexed*, I would link it to *confused*, a word they comprehend.

A Sample Mini-Lesson

Here is how I would go about preteaching the key concept words for a unit on simple machines to a seventh-grade class. Note how the words for the study emerge from these ideas.

Identify the concepts in the chapter:

- Tools, such as levers, pulleys, and wedges, are simple machines.
- Simple machines make hard work much easier.
- Many simple machines developed from levers, pulleys, wheel and axles, and wedges.
- There are three classes of levers, and different machines developed from each class.

Select new words to teach before the class reads the chapter:

1. lever
2. fulcrum
3. effort or load

I draw pictures on chart paper of simple machines, such as a shovel, a wheelbarrow, and a bottle opener. For each picture, I label the three basic parts of levers—lever, fulcrum, and effort or load.

Connect new words to familiar ideas and words:

1. LEVER—a crowbar to loosen a large stone or tree stump from the ground. Show how the lever can lift large amounts of weight; use a bottle opener as a lever to pry open the cap on a bottle of soda.

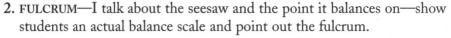

2. FULCRUM—I talk about the seesaw and the point it balances on—show students an actual balance scale and point out the fulcrum.

3. EFFORT OR LOAD—the bottle cap, the weight of children on a seesaw, the dirt in a wheelbarrow, the weight of a stone or tree stump.

STRATEGY IN ACTION

Seventh Graders Draw and Label New Words

After presenting the mini-lesson on *lever*, *fulcrum*, and *effort*, I asked students to explain each new term by creating a labeled drawing of their own, using the three words. This was difficult for many students, but I reassured them that it would lead them to a thorough understanding of these terms. As we read and discussed the chapter over the next five days, students returned to their journals to refine their definitions. Setting aside time to revisit and rethink written explanations allowed students to deepen their understandings of the concepts.

For a culminating activity, I invited students to explain first-, second-, or third-class levers by setting up double-entry pages in their journals. On the left-hand side students had to draw a simple bar that explains the type of lever as well as two labeled examples of simple machines based on the class of lever they chose to explain. Jaime's double-entry journal clearly shows the benefits of giving students many opportunities to work with new words.

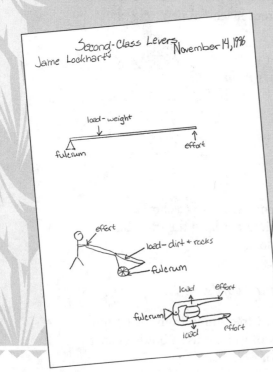

In second-class levers, the fulcrum is at one end of a rod and the effort at the other end. The load—what has to be moved or raised is always between the fulcrum and effort.

A wheel barrow is a good example of a second class lever. A load of dirt or rocks is moved by someone pushing on the handle. The fulcrum is the wheel that rotates.

Another second class lever is a nutcracker. The effort is a hand squeezing the two bars. The nut is the load and the fulcrum is at the end where the 2 handles meet.

When the load is closer to the fulcrum its easier to move it. In the wheel barrow the load is on top of the fulcrum. In the nutcracker the nut is closer to the fulcrum.

▲

This double-entry journal illustrates a seventh grader's knowledge of second-class levers.

Using a Vocabulary Discussion Chart

PURPOSE

to stimulate class discussions about vocabulary that relates to a new topic; to discover what students know about the new words and/or how much they remember

MATERIALS

index cards or large stick-on notes, chart paper, marker pens

SUGGESTIONS FOR PRESENTING YOUR DEMONSTRATION:

1 Record your lesson on large chart paper so you and your students can revisit it during and at the end of your study.

2 Write the topic in the center of the chart.

3 Branching out from the central word, write five to six words that illustrate some key concepts about the topic. In a fourth-grade class studying space, the teacher wrote these words: *astronauts, meteorites, zero gravity,* and *light years*.

4 Conceal the words with index cards or large stick-on notes, taping just the top of the card to the chart.

5 To begin the mini-lesson, flip up one card, read the word, and think aloud, showing students what you recall about that word.

6 Explain to students that it's okay if they know nothing about a word, since the purpose of this strategy to is discover how much information they have.

7 Now flip up the remaining cards one at a time, and invite students to talk about each word.

TIP BOX

Interpreting Discussions

If students discussions reveal that they know a great deal about the vocabulary and topic, quickly review known material, then move on. Sometimes, a group or the entire class has little or no background information. When this is the case, it s crucial that you build some prior knowledge before starting the unit. Without it, comprehension falters. Build prior knowledge by reading aloud, inviting students to look at photographs and illustrations, showing a filmstrip or video, or completing some hands-on activities.

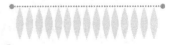

Fourth Graders Complete a Vocabulary Discussion Chart

Before fourth graders study the tropical rain forest, I create a discussion chart. Below it are some of the students' comments for two of the words:

oxygen

tropical animals

felling trees

Tropical Rain Forest

erosion

tropical plants

First Word: *oxygen*

Natasha:	The plants give oxygen to the air.
Shaundra:	I thought plants use oxygen like us.
Robb:	Do you remember the experiment we did with the plant under a glass jar?
Juan:	Yeah. A candle burned brightly in the jar. It had oxygen.
Jimmie:	We took the plant out first.
Shaundra:	So what do plants breathe?
Mike:	Carbon dioxide.
Rosa:	That's the stuff that cars give off from those pipes at the back.
Juan:	You mean exhaust pipes. They also give off carbon monoxide.
Mike:	Uh-huh. Factories and trucks give that off too.

Second Word: *felling [trees]*

Natasha:	I think it means cutting down lots of trees.
Juan:	On the news it once said that cutting all the trees can hurt the land.
Sara:	My dad says that land without trees washes away when it rains hard.
Marvin:	When it really rains, the water makes streams. The streams are muddy.
Monisha:	I bet the insects and animals under the ground drown when it pours.
Natasha:	I bet it makes rivers.
Sal:	It's like when it floods in Virginia. But lots worse.

These snippets of classroom conversations illustrate how students use their experiences, such as a class experiment and what happens on their farms, to connect to vocabulary. What I learned from the discussion is that students knew little about the plant life and animals of the rain forest. They also had no concept of the layers of plant life that reached 120 feet! Students' discussion highlighted concepts we needed to discuss in depth and terms that required clarification. I could also pinpoint information students would readily connect to as they read Jean Craighead George's *One Day in the Tropical Rain Forest* (HarperCollins).

Fifth Graders Meet New Math Terms With a Vocabulary Discussion Chart

Before starting a unit on fractions, the teacher and I developed a vocabulary discussion chart to determine how much students knew about fractions and related concepts. We placed the word *Fractions* in the center of the chart and printed these terms: *least common denominator, rational numbers, numerator, denominator, fractions.*

We invited students to tell us what they knew about the terms. It was an efficient way to pinpoint what students truly understood, what should be carefully retaught, and what information was new.

No one had heard of the term *rational numbers*. Everyone in the class could explain in words and give mathematical examples for all of the terms except *least common denominator.* Below are some fifth graders' comments that reveal their confusion between the *least common denominator* and the *least common multiple*.

Fiona: The least common denominator is the smallest number two numbers have in common.

Stuart: It can't be. How could you add 1/4 and 1/8?

Fiona: I don't know. I don't get it.

Shaundra: I think Fiona meant multiples—like counting by numbers, like 2, 4, 6, 8.

Max: What's the difference between multiples and the least common denominator?

Fiona: What's the point anyway?

Confused by these concepts, students were frustrated and angry. Recognizing their frustration level before initiating the study helped the teacher and me jump in and support students at the outset. Below are some interventions the teacher and I planned to reduce the confusion about least common denominator and least common multiple. Our goal was to improve students' grasp of these concepts early on so they would experience success with more complicated ideas that were in the chapter.

Planned Interventions

- Offer hands-on experiences to help them with these concepts.
- Explore with students the purpose of knowing this information.
- Have students work in pairs to explain the concepts to each other, using manipulatives.
- Have students write about each concept in their math journals, giving examples that illustrate each, and point to differences.
- Review several times throughout the unit.

▲ *Fifth graders present their vocabulary discussion chart to classmates.*

The What-Do-I-Know Strategy

Like the Vocabulary Discussion Chart, this strategy is also ideal for building vocabulary in mathematics, social studies, and science. Students generate and categorize words prior to a study, then adjust meanings throughout the theme. As students share ideas, you accrue a rich vocabulary list on the chart. For example, when fifth graders and I began a unit on bats, some students shared words such as *sonar, guano, vegetarian, nocturnal*—words that many students were unfamiliar with. However, discussing these words before reading enriched every child's background knowledge.

What makes this a great strategy are the three follow-up questions you pose—questions that invite students to think deeply about their learning:

1. What do I want to know more about?

Ask this question after students preview a chapter by studying charts and pictures, and reading captions and bold face words and headings. Record their suggestions on chart paper.

2. What have I learned about this topic?

During and after the study, ask students to brainstorm, in their journals, a list of what they have learned. Share and discuss items with the entire class. In addition to information, students will also learn about the vocabulary associated with a topic.

3. How did I go about learning this information?

This is an invitation for students to reflect on their process and strategies. Have students respond to this question in their journals. Set aside time for students to exchange their ideas and share what worked.

◄ ◄ ◄ ◄ ◄ ◄ ◄ ◄ ◄ ◄ ◄ ◄ ◄   ► ► ► ► ► ► ► ► ► ► ► ► ►

What Do I Know?

PURPOSE

to clarify the meanings of words; to collect words related to a topic or a new word; to discover what students already know, so you can decide what to review and what to emphasize

MATERIALS

chart paper, marker pens

SUGGESTIONS FOR PRESENTING YOUR DEMONSTRATION:

1 Write a question on the chalkboard, such as "What do you know about multiplication?"

2 Talk about the topic and list what you recall.

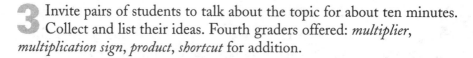

3 Invite pairs of students to talk about the topic for about ten minutes. Collect and list their ideas. Fourth graders offered: *multiplier, multiplication sign, product, shortcut* for addition.

4 Explain to students that you will use this strategy at other points during the unit to discover what they know about the topic or word the class will be studying.

Steps for Organizing a What-Do-I-Know Discussion

First Day:

1. Organize students into pairs or groups of four.
2. Invite groups to spend 10 minutes discussing what they know about a topic, such as *geometry, civil rights, earthworm farms,* etc.
3. Have students write all they recall on a journal page headed with each student's name, date, and the topic.
4. Ask groups to select a spokesperson to share their discussion.
5. Record, on chart paper, the key information each group shares.
6. Call for questions about the information, and record these on the chart.
7. Have students copy in their journals key terms that you select from the chart.

Second Day:

1. Ask students to develop categories for the items on the chart. Fifth graders created these categories for "What Do You Know About Bats?": Appearance, Habitat, Food, Behavior, Legends, How Helpful to Man.

While Students Are Immersed in a Study:

1. Invite students to explain four to five key terms.
2. Set aside some time for students to refine their explanations.
3. Fine-tune explanations at the end of the study.

By giving students responsibility for exploring and refining their understanding of vocabulary, they are more apt to integrate these words into their reading, writing, and speaking vocabularies.

Seventh Graders Use the What-Do-I-Know Technique

At the outset of a study of geometry, seventh graders shared what they knew about the topic. It was the ideal time for students to pinpoint terms they understood and terms that were new. Throughout the study, the class revisited the chart, refining original explanations of terms and ideas.

Seventh-Grade Chart on What Do We Know About Geometry?

- plane geometry
- vertical angle
- right triangle
- acute angle
- parallel lines
- perimeter
- *pi*

- solid geometry
- intersecting lines
- isosceles triangle
- equilateral triangle
- perpendicular
- area
- radius, diameter

Here is the progression of explanations from a student's journal. Note how this student moved from a superficial understanding to a deeper one.

Word: *pi*

Before Reading: It's a Greek word and the Greeks invented it. It's a fraction, but I don't remember the parts.

While Reading and Discussing: It shows the ratio of the circumference of a circle to the diameter of a circle. It is 3.1459+. The Greeks invented it.

After Completing the Unit: The ratio—*pi*—is the same for all circles—the smallest to the biggest you can think of. The diameter is the line that passes through the center of a circle. You can also write *pi* as a fraction—22/7. *Ratio* means the relationship between the circumference and the diameter.

Not only did students gain deeper insights into *pi*, but they also used, with more confidence, these mathematical terms: *diameter, ratio, circumference, fraction.*

Browsing for New Words

This is a great follow-up activity to the "Vocabulary Discussion Web" and the "What Do You Know?" strategy. It's especially useful when students exhibit that they *don't* understand the concepts and vocabulary you're introducing.

PURPOSE

to build vocabulary and prior knowledge before students study a topic by browsing through a chapter or books

MATERIALS

a chapter in a textbook or several nonfiction books on a topic; one to two pages of a text that has boldface words and pictures with captions; chart paper; marker pens; an overhead projector; a transparency

SUGGESTIONS FOR PRESENTING YOUR DEMONSTRATION:

1 Make a transparency of the pages you've selected, and place on an overhead projector.

2 Model how you browse through these pages. Read aloud the main headings and sentences that include the words in boldface; study pictures and graphs and read captions.

3 List on chart paper two to three unfamiliar words.

4 Read aloud each sentence that contains one of the new words.

5 Write the word on the chart paper, and try to explain it in your own words, pointing out the clues you used to figure out the word's meaning.

6 Reread the passage. Refine the meaning of the word.

Steps for Organizing the New Word Search Strategy

1. After the mini-lesson, organize students into pairs.

2. Have partners browse through the text for 10 to 15 minutes and identify new words.

3. Ask students to record unfamiliar words in their journals.

4. Collect the words on chart paper. (During the study, reserve five to 10 minutes several times a week for students to discuss the charted words and refine their understandings.)

5. Toward the end of a study, invite students to explain the meanings of four to five words in their journals. I usually select one or two words and let students choose one or two. Don't give in to the urge to ask students to explain 10 to 12 words. It's tedious and unnecessary. By revisiting, refining, and using new words, students have already gained a deeper knowledge of the new vocabulary.

Frequently invite students to explore words in the dictionary, and you may just inspire in them a lifelong fascination with words.

▼

Seventh Graders Chart
Their New Word Search

After browsing through the geometry chapter in their textbook, seventh graders culled these words on chart paper:

Seventh Graders' Chart After the New Word Search

- transversal
- bisector
- congruent
- Pythagorean theorem

- area of a circle
- tangent
- scalene triangle
- isosceles triangles

Later in the unit, their teacher asked them to explain the Pythagorean theorem with words and drawings. Then students chose a term to explain in writing.

First I made 4 right triangles with legs of 4cm by 5cm. I put them together to form a square in the middle. When I measured each side of the square with a ruler, it came out to be 6.4cm.

I can figure out the side of the square using the Pythagorean theorem. The theorem only works with right triangles. The sides of a right triangle are called legs, the line that joins the legs is the hypotenuse. This is the theorem— $a^2 + b^2 = c^2$

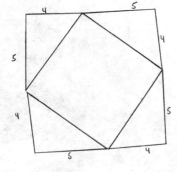

$4^2 + 5^2 = c^2$
$16 + 25 = 41$
$c = \sqrt{41}$
$c = 6.4$
I used the calculator to figure out the square root.

The square root was the same as when I measured it with a ruler.

If you know any two measurements of a right triangle you can figure out the third side using the Pythagorean theorem.

lets say $a = 1$ $a^2 = 1$
$b = 2$ $b^2 = 2$
$c = 2\frac{1}{4}$ $c^2 = ?$
← used ruler

Pythagoros says $a^2 + b^2 = c^2$

$1 + 4 = 5$
$c = \sqrt{5}$
use calculator $c = 2.24$

Math journals are an important tool for students. Although the entry of the stronger math student (left) illustrates a greater understanding, the weaker student has also gained important insights from ongoing class discussions.

Develop Students' Knowledge of Word Parts

Word parts or roots come from other languages such as Latin, Greek, German, and Old French. Knowing the meanings of common roots enables learners to sleuth out the meaning of unfamiliar words. Annie, a seventh grader, figured out the meaning of *soliloquy* because she knew the definition of these Latin word parts: *loquence*, which means speaking, and *soli* which means alone. In her journal she wrote, "A *soliloquy* is speaking alone, like a character in a play who speaks what's inside. It comes from two Latin roots—*loquence*—talk—and *soli*—alone." (See list of roots in appendix, pages 90–93.)

Students often confuse the term *base word* with roots or stems. A *base word* is a word stripped of prefixes and suffixes that can stand as a word. For example, by removing *dis* and *ed* from *disregarded*, the base word *regard* remains; but by removing *inter* and *ed* from *interfered*, the Latin root *fer*, meaning "to bear or carry," remains.

Studying prefixes and suffixes offers students these benefits:

※ They can use their knowledge of prefixes, suffixes, and roots to segment words and say parts of words that stump them. A fourth grader who stumbled over *unintelligible* returned to the word and said, *un–in–tell*— and then she put the parts together.

※ Knowing the meanings of prefixes and suffixes can support students as they try to determine the meaning of a new word. Here's how a seventh grader reasoned the meaning of *impenetrable*: "*im* means *not*, *penetrate* is the base word and means *cut through*, so I have *not penetrate*—the suffix *able* means *shows an effect*. *Impenetrable* means not able to cut through. It is an adjective."

STANDARDIZED TEST LINK

Once students know the meanings of many roots, prefixes, and suffixes, they can use their knowledge to figure out the meaning of unfamiliar words in reading passages where context clues befuddle them and in analogies for which they don t know the meanings of some of the choices. When confronted with a word and four choices, like the sample below, a knowledge of word parts helped sixth grader Shantell pick the best meaning for *epidemic*.

An epidemic is

(a) an illness   **(b)** a contagious disease   **(c)** anything spread rapidly   **(d)** prevalent

Shantell reasoned: The prefix *epi* means *upon*, and the root *demos* means *people*. Shantell chose (*c*), because the prefix and root didn t have disease in it. Anything could be an epidemic as long as lots of people were involved, she explained.

Prefixes and Suffixes

PURPOSE

to teach students the meanings of prefixes and suffixes so they can pronounce unfamiliar words and figure out their meanings; to show how suffixes often determine whether a word is a noun, adjective, or adverb

MATERIALS

two to three prefixes and/or suffixes you have selected; five to 10 base words that come from students' reading, writing, and spelling; chart paper; marker pens

SUGGESTIONS FOR PRESENTING YOUR DEMONSTRATION:

1 Write the prefixes, suffixes, and their meanings on chart paper. In a mini-lesson for eighth graders, I used: *in*, *dis*, *re*, *ly*, and *tion*.

2 Print four to six base words that emerged from students' studies. During an eighth grade study of prejudice, I wrote: *credible*, *connect*, *incredible*, and *equal*.

3 Use the prefixes and/or suffixes and one to two base words to create new words. I wrote: *reconnect*

4 Invite students to build words using the remaining base words. For example, my students created: *disconnect*, *disconnection*, *equally*, *inequality*.

5 Think aloud and explain the meaning of each word using your knowledge of prefixes and suffixes. Here's my think-aloud for *disconnection*: "The prefix, *dis* means *the opposite of*; *connect* means *joined*, *together*, or *related*; and *tion* is a suffix that indicates a noun. *Disconnection* means *not related* or *joined*."

6 Point out how suffixes help you identify a word's part of speech.

TIP BOX

Gear Up for Grammar

Suffix studies support grammar. Once students see that endings of words can signal a noun, adjective, adverb, or verbal form, they're on the lookout for these clues. For example, eighth graders noticed that the suffix *tion* signaled a noun, and *ly* an adverb. (See a list of prefixes and suffixes on page 95.)

Eighth Graders Present Prefixes and Suffixes

By January, my eighth graders have a solid knowledge of prefixes and suffixes. To support their study of economics in history, I printed a list of words on chart paper, divided students into groups of four, and asked them to build sets of related words. Over the next four days, members of each group took turns presenting their words, explaining meanings and parts of speech. Here is what one group did with its set of words:

Base Word	Related Words and Their Parts of Speech
annual	annually (adv.), biannual (noun, adj.)
finance	financial (adj.), financing (pres. participle), refinance (verb)
invest	investing (pres. participle), reinvest (verb), investment (noun, adj.)

Eighth graders work on their word list.

Teaching Word Parts

PURPOSE

to build, for students, knowledge of roots, prefixes, and suffixes so they can use this knowledge to figure out the meaning of new words

MATERIALS

a root that's related to your studies in language arts or a content-area subject; chart paper, marker pens

SUGGESTIONS FOR PRESENTING YOUR DEMONSTRATION:

First Day:

1 Organize students into pairs or groups of four.

2 Give each group two dictionaries.

3 Write the root, its meaning, and the language it comes from on top of a chart. Sixth graders worked with the Latin root, *circum.*

4 Invite groups to brainstorm a list of words that they think come from this root. Each student records the group's words in a journal. One sixth grader wrote these words in her journal: *circumference, circumnavigate,* and *circumstances.*

5 Have pairs or groups check their words in the dictionary to make sure the word comes from the root. (See page 40 for a mini-lesson on using the dictionary.)

6 Challenge students to find two to three additional dictionary words that come from the root. One pair discovered *circumspect, circumvent,* and *circumscribe.*

Second Day:

1 Collect students' words on chart paper. Have students volunteer to explain the meanings of the words, using their knowledge of the root, prefixes, and suffixes.

2 Have students write in their journals any words from the chart that were not on their lists.

Third Day:

1 Discuss the part of speech of each word.

Fourth Day:

1 Model on chart paper how each word functions in a sentence, or select words that are developmentally appropriate for your students.

2 Have students create sentences in their journals that demonstrate their ability to use the word in a meaningful context. For *circumnavigate*, one pair wrote this sentence: The space probe took photographs as it *circumnavigated* the moon.

3 Collect sample sentences from students and record on chart paper.

Dictionary Dipping

P U R P O S E

to teach students how to locate the origin of a word in a dictionary

M A T E R I A L S

dictionaries, journals, large chart paper, marker pens

SUGGESTIONS FOR PRESENTING YOUR DEMONSTRATION:

On large chart paper, I record the part of a dictionary entry which includes the word's origin:

por' tal, *n.* [ME.; OFr.; ML. *portale*, orig.neut. of *portalis*, of a door, from L. *porta*, gate.]

im port', *v.t.*; imported, *pt., pp.*; importing, *ppr.* [L. *importare*, to bring in, introduce, bring about; *in*, in, and *portare*, to carry.]

Robb s Mini-Lesson

[The students and I have already studied what can be learned from the boldface entry word in a dictionary, abbreviations of parts of speech, and the different forms of verbs.]

I tell students the following:

  "All the information about the origin of *portal* you'll find inside the brackets. [I point to the brackets.] In the front of your dictionaries, on page xi, is a list of abbreviations. You'll see that ME stands for Middle English, OFr for Old French, ML for Medieval Latin, and L for Latin. Since we know that *port* is a Latin root, I'll check its meaning. *Portal* comes from a Latin word meaning *gate* and is not related to the root *port*, meaning *to carry*. I wrote *import* on the chart so you can study a word that **does** come from the Latin root meaning *to carry*. "

Now I call for students' questions and observations. Here are some of their comments and my reponses:

Students: Why do they give you all the other languages?

Response: To show you that the root was part of several languages. It was confusing having <u>port</u> in both and yet they have different meanings. Now we can see why.

Students: Do the brackets come so close to the entry word in all dictionaries?

Response: The brackets come after the parts of speech have been named.

Students: What does <u>im</u> mean?

Response: The prefix <u>im</u> is an assimilated form of <u>in</u>, meaning <u>not</u>. <u>Im</u> is used before <u>b</u> (<u>imbecile</u>), <u>m</u> (<u>immortal</u>), and <u>p</u> (<u>important</u>).

Students: Can you find <u>im</u> in the dictionary?

Response: Yes, You'll find it's just before the list of words starting with <u>im</u>.

STRATEGY IN ACTION

Fifth Graders Dictionary Dip

After discussing students' questions, I invite them to select two words from the list of words related to *port*. Because I have accepted all students' suggestions, I must provide time for students to check the words and their roots in the dictionary. Students create two columns of words: The first lists words related to the root *port*, the second, words related to a different root.

One pair of fifth graders points out that they learned that *portend* comes from the Latin *portendere* meaning *to foretell*; another pair discover that *portico* comes from the Latin words *porticus* and *porta*, meaning *door*.

By encouraging students to generate all the words they think are related to a particular root and then inviting pairs to check the list, students broaden their vocabulary and get acqainted with other roots. "I never thought words could be so interesting," one fifth grader told me. My goal is to create enthusiasm for etymology early on, so by eighth grade, students naturally turn to the dictionary to explore words and their roots.

◄◄◄◄◄◄◄◄◄◄◄◄   ▶▶▶▶▶▶▶▶▶▶▶▶

Webbing Words From Roots

PURPOSE

to expand students' vocabulary within content-area topics

MATERIALS

dictionaries, overhead projector, blank transparencies, marker pens

SUGGESTIONS FOR PRESENTING YOUR DEMONSTRATION:

1 Select a root that relates to students' studies.

2 Print the root, its meaning, and origin in the center of a transparency for overhead projectors. Place a circle around the root information.

3 Brainstorm words related to the root and record these so they branch out from the circle. Keep related words, such as *transport*, *transporting*, *transportation*, and *transported*, in the same cluster.

4 Search for more words in the textbook or a free-choice reading book.

5 Model how you use the dictionary to check your words and discover two to three additional words such as *transfer* and *transact*.

Sixth Graders Web Words From Roots

*I*n math class, sixth graders were studying and creating polygons. To extend students' vocabulary, their teacher and I organized 18 students into six groups and invited them to create a web of words related to these word parts: *penta, octo, deca, hexa, nona,* and *octa.* After using the dictionary and math textbooks as resources, groups created webs on an overhead transparency sheet and presented their findings to the class.

A sixth grader's web for the Latin root, penta. ▶

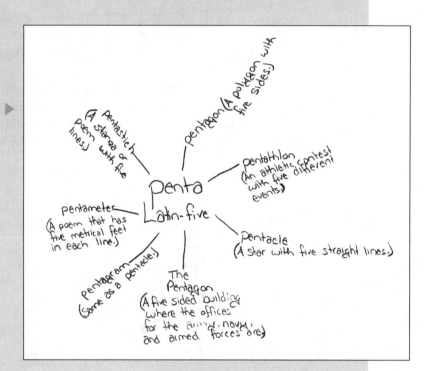

Steps for Doing the Word Web Activity in Your Classroom

To conduct this activity, follow these steps:

1. Organize students into groups of four.

2. Have each group choose a scribe to record the root, its meaning, and origin in the center of an overhead transparency (or chart paper) and then circle it.

3. Tell groups to spend about 15 minutes brainstorming and searching for words related to the roots in their textbooks. Instruct them to discuss each word they constructed, so they can explain the meanings of all the words.

4. Have them check each new word in the dictionary to ensure that each word comes from each group's stem.

5. Have them write new words so that they radiate from the stem. Keep related words in the same cluster.

6. When the groups are finished, have them take turns presenting their findings. They can place transparencies on an overhead projector or tape the chart paper to the blackboard.

7. Encourage each group member to explain at least one word to the class. Listeners, including the teacher, can add information or raise questions.

The Predict-and-Clarify Strategy

With this strategy, you'll encourage students to use their knowledge of word parts and some information from a text to predict the meaning of unfamiliar words. It's great for struggling readers, because it slowly builds prior knowledge and ultimately improves comprehension of new material.

You'll find this strategy especially effective in science, math, and social studies, where students are often bombarded with new concepts and a long list of unfamiliar words. The samples I've included were composed by three students in fifth grade and a group of four students in fourth grade.

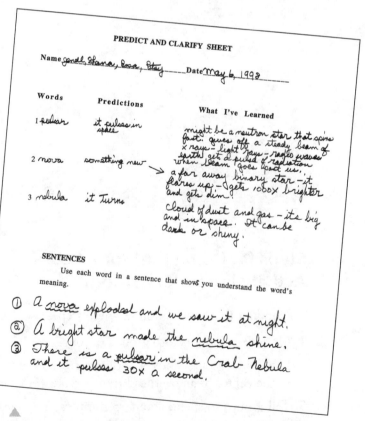

Fifth graders clarify their predictions after reading about the nervous system.

A team of fourth graders can use new words in sentences after clarifying and discussing their meanings.

STANDARDIZED TEST LINK

Encourage students to use the prediction strategy when a word on a test seems unfamiliar. Students who score high on standardized vocabulary tests use these strategies that relate to predicting:

- Try to use clues in the passage that will help you predict and ask questions such as, Is the meaning restated? Is there an example that provides a clue? Do sentences that come before and after contain clues?

- Think of a discussion where you might have used the word to describe a character or an event. Practicing the strategy with my books really helped me, eighth grader Elvis told me. That s how I remembered *impetuous*. David, in our book group, used that word to describe Gilly s decision to steal Mr. Randolph s money.

- Use your knowledge of prefixes, suffixes, roots, and parts of speech to predict a word s meaning. For example, Shauna, a seventh grader, used her knowledge of prefixes to figure out the meaning of *interlocution*. I know inter means between and I recalled how you [Mrs. Robb] always tell us we re loquacious, so I think it must be talk between people.

Predict and Clarify

PURPOSE

to predict the meaning of words based on a preview of pages; to refine and clarify meanings as the section is read and discussed; to have students revisit and adjust a word s meaning many times

MATERIALS

textbook; four to five preselected words; chart paper; marker pens

SUGGESTIONS FOR PRESENTING YOUR DEMONSTRATION:

1 Print on chart paper these headings for three columns:

Words, **Predictions**, and **What I Have Learned**

First Day:

2 List under **Words** four to five words students need to know to understand the concepts in a chapter or section. Leave several lines between words. Before introducing seventh graders to a a section on mixtures and solutions, Ray Legge, a middle school science teacher, wrote these words on the chart: *heterogeneous mixture, homogeneous mixture, solution,* and *colloid.*

3 Locate the first word in the text, and read aloud the sentence that contains that word. Mr. Legge read: "A mixture in which different materials are spread out unevenly is called a heterogeneous mixture."

4 Think out loud, explaining your prediction of the word's meaning and the clues you used. Here's what Mr. Legge said: "It says a heterogeneous mixture is made of different materials. The materials are spread out evenly."

5 Record your prediction on the chart.

6 Read aloud the entire section containing the word. Think out loud, sharing with students additional information you picked up. Here's the additional information Mr. Legge added: "Examples of a heterogeneous mixture are gravel, concrete, and dry soups."

7 List these ideas under the **What I Have Learned** column.

8 After students ask questions about the mini-lesson, invite them to help you predict the meaning of the remaining words. (See Tip Box, page 47.)

Second Day:

1 Have students read the chapter and discuss information.

2 Ask students to adjust predictions. Print these under **What I Have Learned**. Students added this idea: "It's easy to spot a heterogeneous mixture because you can see, with your eyes, the different materials, such as dried onion, carrots, peas, and noodles, in the soup."

At the Close of the Study:

1 Have students refine their adjustments, using all the knowledge they've gained during the study.

Steps for Organizing Students for the Predict-and-Clarify Strategy

Give students a copy of the Predict and Clarify Sheet (page 48). Organize students in pairs or groups of three to four. Have students record preselected words on their Predict and Clarify Sheet. Then ask students to do the following:

1. Skim the pages for each boldface word.

Learning benefit: Students develop the ability to quickly look through several pages for specific words or phrases.

2. Read the sentence that contains the word.

Learning benefit: Students start to familiarize themselves with the content.

3. Discuss the meaning of the word with your partner or group.

Learning benefit: Sharing allows students to support one another as they try to learn more about an unfamiliar word.

4. Predict the word's meaning based on the sentence and your group's discussion.

Learning benefit: By asking students to predict, you are not looking for a correct response. At this stage, students are learning about new words through active involvement and collaboration.

5. Partners or groups share their predictions with classmates.

Learning benefit: Students expand their knowledge and understanding of these words by listening to everyone's ideas.

Now have students read the selection, discuss it, and return to clarify their predictions. Under **What I Have Learned**, invite students to fine-tune their explanations of each word. You can have them continue refining and adding to their definitions throughout the study. As a culminating activity, students can write sentences using the words to show they understand the meanings.

Predict and Clarify Sheet

Words	Predictions	What I've Learned
1		
2		
3		

Sentences

Use each word in a sentence to show that you understand the word's meaning.

With this sheet, students can deepen their understanding of new words.

Closing Reflections

Over the years, I've learned how crucial it is for me to determine what my students know and don't know about a topic. The less they know, the more opportunities they need to fill their knowledge-and-experience tanks so they can cope with new information and many unfamiliar words.

Before introducing themes to students, I always challenge myself to consider the questions that follow. Reflecting on these questions guarantees that I will set aside enough class time to prepare students for learning.

❋ How much prior knowledge and experience do my students have?

❋ Have I given them enough experiences before reading?

❋ Have I taken the time to preteach key vocabulary?

❋ Did I offer many opportunities for students to talk and share?

❋ Have I listened carefully to students' responses in order to evaluate their readiness to plunge into unfamiliar territory?

Improving Vocabulary While Reading

> ❝I want to stop reading when someone says, 'Look it up in the dictionary.' I need ways to figure out the meaning without stopping for a long time.❞
>
> —*Seventh Grader*

"Look it up in the dictionary," my parents and teachers often said when I hit a word in my reading that baffled me. It was advice that was easier said than done. The truth is, looking words up is not always sage advice. It interrupts the flow of reading. Often the desire to continue reading diminishes or disappears, and readers set aside a book. So what can we offer students in lieu of a trip to the dictionary? We can model for them how to access a problem-solving strategy that will reveal a word's meaning in moments. In this chapter, you will find strategies that resolve the three kinds of vocabulary difficulties students encounter while reading:

Students figure out a word's meaning with context clues.

1. They can pronounce the word, but the meaning befuddles them.

2. They cannot say the word, but once they figure out the pronunciation, they can determine the word's meaning.

3. They cannot say the word, and they don't know and can't figure out its meaning.

Outfitted with problem-solving strategies, students can pause briefly, solve a problem, and continue enjoying their book. The strategies that follow can lead to independence in reading. Such tools build students' word knowledge and teach them to use clues authors embed in a text to understand a word's meaning.

Noting Words That Baffle

Often, struggling and reluctant readers lack the strategies for figuring out the pronunciation and/or meaning of unfamiliar words. Give students stick-on notes or a bookmark—just a strip of paper cut in half lengthwise—and ask them to jot down the page number and the word that stumped them. When the same word stumps everyone, you might want to present a mini-lesson for the entire class (see page 51 for mini-lesson). More often, you'll work with pairs or small groups of students.

STANDARDIZED TEST LINK

Once you get students practicing and using strategies that help them figure out new words, they'll have the tools for decoding unfamiliar words. Frequently, when students can say a new word, they know its meaning because it has been used at school and at home or in a movie or T.V. show. While students reread a passage to help them say the new word, they're also finding clues that can clarify its meaning. Salvadore pointed out that on a teacher-made practice vocabulary test he read the following sentence three times, skipping *gregarious* and reading to the end: *The old woman had a* gregarious *nature, for she was happiest when she was talking to and doing things with people.* Then Sal looked for small, familiar words, like the name *Greg* and parts of words he could pronounce, like *ous*, before he tried to blend parts he knew and say *gregarious*: "As soon as I said [the word], it was easy. I knew from clues like 'she was happiest with people' that the best choice was *sociable*."

Reserve time for students to share with classmates how they figure out the pronunciation of a new word. Hearing how others solve this common problem will increase students' menu of strategies.

◄◄◄◄◄◄◄◄◄◄◄◄◄   ►►►►►►►►►►►►►►

Strategies to Use When You're Stuck on a Word

PURPOSE

to provide practice with strategies that help students pronounce unfamiliar and/or multisyllable words

MATERIALS

students' reading book, hard-to-pronounce words students and/or teacher have identified

SUGGESTIONS FOR PRESENTING YOUR DEMONSTRATION:

1 Select two to three words from a book you are reading aloud or one that students are reading.

2 Write one of the words and the sentence it's part of on the blackboard. The word and sentence I wrote were from *Chameleons on Location* by Kathy Darling.

Word: *deceptions*
Sentence: Scientists call their little *deceptions* disinformation.

3 Think aloud, showing how you say, then remove, the prefix and suffix; then, look at the root or base word.

4 Pronounce the root or base word, then add the prefix and pronounce it. Finally, add the suffix and pronounce it.

5 Reread the sentence with the word to check if it makes sense.

6 Put the second sentence and word on the board. The word and sentence I used were from *Jacob Have I Loved* by Katherine Paterson.

Word: *drudgery*
Sentence: This was a day for adventure, not *drudgery*.

TIP BOX

Who Are Those Struggling or Reluctant Readers?

Struggling or at-risk readers are comfortable in texts that are several years below their grade level. Reading is painful and unpleasant, and these students have not developed personal reading lives. Struggling readers have limited vocabularies, experience difficulty with decoding multisyllable words, and lack fluency and the strategies that enable them to get interested in books and solve problems about print as they read.

Reluctant readers are good readers, but only read to complete school assignments. They possess solid strategies and skills. Rarely do they choose reading during free time at home or in school.

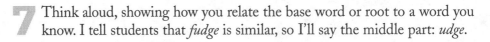

7 Think aloud, showing how you relate the base word or root to a word you know. I tell students that *fudge* is similar, so I'll say the middle part: *udge*.

8 Put the parts together and reread the sentence.

9 Write the third word and sentence on the blackboard. Ask for a volunteer to use one of the processes you modeled.

10 Give each student a copy of the strategy sheet and discuss it. Students can store the guidelines in their reading journals or folders.

11 Have students practice the strategy in pairs. Each child chooses three to four tough words from a reading book. Students support one another as they try to say each word.

STRATEGY IN ACTION

Fourth Graders Use When-You're-Stuck-on-a-Word Strategies

Sandi and Shaundra are reading *Return to Sender* by Kevin Henkes. Scrunched together on a bean-bag chair at the back of their classroom, I observe the girls helping each other with words that stump them. The pair have read to page 50, talked about the book, and now return to pages marked with stick-on notes to check up on the pronunciation of some words.

Sandi points to the words *unfocused* and *blurred* in this sentence on page 40: *He peered down at the tiny jewels until,* unfocused, *they* blurred *his vision.*

She reads *unfocused* as *un* and stops. Next, she tries *blurred* and reads it as *blotted*. Shaundra has Sandi say, then remove, the *un* and *ed* in *unfocused*, and tells Sandi the base word "is easy because it sounds like hocus-pocus." Quickly, Sandi says the base word and adds the prefix and suffix. Now Shaundra points to the double *r's* in *blurred* and tells Sandi she read those as *t*. Though *blotted* and *blurred* both work in this sentence, Shaundra helps Sandi, who tends to guess sounds in unfamiliar words, attend to the middle of the word.

In addition to mini-lessons where students observe me solving similar problems, students practice decoding strategies with a partner or in groups of three or four. I circulate among groups, responding immediately to those who request help. In their journals, students keep a copy of these strategies to refer to as they attempt to pronounce words that pose problems.

Using the Clues Authors Provide

When authors use more sophisticated words, they frequently embed clues so the reader can determine the words' meanings. In mini-lessons, using books students are reading, demonstrate how each of the clues that follow work. I've included examples from fiction and nonfiction. (See pages 55–57.)

Periodically invite students to provide examples of each type of clue from their reading. Extending such invitations provides the practice from books that students require in order to develop a knowledge of these contextual clues.

※ **A Clear Definition:** The word's meaning follows phrases such as *or* or *is called*, or a comma, or dash. (Present to grades 4–8.)

Example: Mongoose slid full-body to the floor. The ceiling was spinning, he was *woozy*. (p. 21, *The Library Card* by Jerry Spinelli, Scholastic)

※ **A Concrete Example:** The reader can decipher the word's meaning by reflecting on the example that has been provided. Examples can be found in a new sentence or following these words or phrases: *for example, such as, like,* and *especially*. (Present to grades 4–8.)

Examples are in the second sentence: Lunch was a *culinary* and *conversational failure*. Dried beef strips, garnished with water cress from the fringes of spring, and monosyllabic responses from Touchstone. (p. 238. *Sabriel* by Garth Nix, HarperCollins, 1995)

※ **Restated Meanings:** Sometimes the author explains a difficult word by restating its meaning in simpler terms. Often, commas set off the meaning from the word. You'll also find restatement after words and phrases such as *or, that is,* and *in other words*. (Present to grades 4–8.)

Example: The sun's surface is called the *photosphere*, a sea of boiling gases about 10,000 degrees (F). (*Our Solar System* by Seymour Simon, Morrow)

※ **Words or Phrases That Modify:** Sometimes modifiers such as adjectives, adverbs, or relative clauses contain clues to a word's meaning. A relative clause begins with *who, which, that, whose,* or *whom* and often explains or extends an idea or word in the main part of a sentence. (Present to grades 6–8.)

Example: The city buzzed with *rumors* that Caesar was planning to make himself king, with Cleopatra as his queen, and that the capital would be moved to Alexandria. (*Cleopatra* by Diane Stanley, Morrow)

Strategies to Use When You're Stuck on a Word

※ Skip the word, read to the end of the sentence. Now reread the sentence.

※ Carefully look at the beginning, middle, and end of the word. Use your knowledge of letter-sound relationships and the sentence's meaning to try to pronounce it.

※ Instead of guessing, reread the sentence containing the word you don't know, as well as the sentences that come before and after it.

※ Try to find clues in those sentences to help you figure out the word.

If that doesn't work...

※ Look closely at the word.

※ If the word has a prefix, try to say it, then take it off.

※ If the word has a suffix, try to say it, then take it off.

※ Look at the base or root word that's left. Does it resemble another word you know? For example, the base *felon* resembles *melon*. Try saying the base word, then blend all the word parts together.

※ Reread the sentence and see if the word makes sense.

If that doesn't work...

※ Ask a classmate or adult for help.

※ Look the word up in the dictionary.

The handwritten chart reads:

Jan. 5, 1998

Clues Writers Leave

1. A clear definition: The word's meaning follows phrases: or, is called, a comma, or a dash.

2. A concrete _____ is given that helps you decipher the word's meaning. Examples follow: such as, like, especially or a new sentence.

An eighth grader reviews the strategy called "A Clear Definition" before classmates search their books for examples.

Watch Those Conjunctions: Coordinating and subordinating conjunctions show relationships and allow readers to link unknown ideas to known ones. *And, but, or, nor, for,* and *yet* are coordinating conjunctions. Common subordinating conjunctions are *since, even though, if, just as, when, whenever,* and *because.* (Present to grades 6-8.)

Example: Cleopatra *captivated* Antony, *just as* she had Julius Caesar. (*Cleopatra* by Diane Stanley, Morrow)

Repetition of the New Word: Often a difficult word is repeated in familiar and different contexts or situations, allowing readers to construct the word's meaning based on what he already knows. (Present to grades 4–8.)

Example: America is a nation of *immigrants. Immigrants* are people who come to a new land to make their home. All Americans are related to *immigrants* or are *immigrants* themselves. (*Coming To America: The Story of Immigration* by Betsy Maestro, Scholastic)

Hot on the Trail of Author Clues

PURPOSE

to raise students awareness of clues authors leave that can help them figure out the meanings of words

MATERIALS

one of the strategies listed on pages 53—54, chart paper, marker pens, students free-choice reading books and/or a textbook, or the novel a class is studying

SUGGESTIONS FOR PRESENTING YOUR DEMONSTRATION:

First Day

1 Print the technique and the example on chart paper.

2 Read and explain the strategy, and tell students how it can help them deal with unfamiliar words.

3 Read the example. Think aloud, explaining how you figure out the meaning of the word.

Second Day

1 Invite students to skim their books and find an example of the technique. In their journals, ask students to print the book's title, the sentence, and the page number.

2 Have students read their sentences and explain how they determined the words' meanings.

3 Continue inviting students to find examples of the technique as they read in science, history, and reading workshop.

STANDARDIZED TEST LINK

*I*f you train your students to be word detectives, unfamiliar vocabulary on tests won't frighten them—they'll be armed with a set of strategies that can unravel the meanings. When a word on a standardized test is in a sentence or a paragraph, there are always clues that can help learners figure out the word's meaning. Teach students to ask these questions:

Does the situation supply clues?
<u>Example:</u> Having the flu for two weeks *enervated* the boy.

Is there a comparison?
<u>Example:</u> Her dress was as *flamboyant* as a peacock's feathers.

Do sentences that come before or after supply clues?
<u>Example:</u> The streets of the medieval town were teeming with rats. Every living person knew the area was *infested* and feared the plague.

For Struggling Readers

1 Ask three to four students to print their journal entries on the chalkboard each day.

2 Have each student explain how she used the clues to discover the word's meaning.

STRATEGY IN ACTION

Fifth Graders Sleuth Author's Clues

During 20 minutes of reading workshop, students discuss examples from books they're reading of two writing techniques: "A Concrete Example" and "Words or Phrases That Modify." On the chalkboard, students write their examples, explain how they deciphered the words' meanings, then invite classmates to comment.

Jake used these sentences from Seymour Simon's *Earthquakes* (Morrow) to illustrate a concrete example:

Yet a million times each year—an average of once every 30 seconds— somewhere around the world the ground shakes and sways. We call this an earthquake.

Students quickly pointed out that the example—*the ground shakes and sways*—came before the word *earthquake*, making it easier to understand this term. One student thought that Simon made sure everyone understood the word *earthquake* immediately because that was what the book was about.

Annie had just completed *The Library Card* by Jerry Spinelli (Scholastic). The sentence, from page 40, that she wrote on the board illustrated a phrase that contained an explanation of *tickbird*.

And a bird, called the tickbird, *that hitches a ride on the back of a rhino.*

Immediately, one student said that this was also an example of "A Clear Definition," because Spinelli used the word *called* to tell exactly what kind of bird it was. "It's easy to know what a tickbird is all about," says Annie, "because he [Spinelli] tells you after the word that."

By reserving time for students to share examples from their own reading, you familiarize them with contextual clues in texts.

Using Vocabulary in Context

PURPOSE

to show students how to sleuth out a word's meaning by finding clues in the sentence and sentences that come before or after the unknown word, and in illustrations, diagrams, photographs, and charts

MATERIALS

overhead transparency and projector; sample sentences from a textbook or reading book

SUGGESTIONS FOR PRESENTING YOUR DEMONSTRATION:

1 On the transparency or chart paper, print three to four difficult sentences and/or passages that you've taken from students' reading. (See copy of sample transparency on page 59.)

2 Uncover each sample one at a time.

3 Read the sample and think aloud, showing students how you use clues to determine a word's meaning. Here's what I told students: "The clues for *wretched conditions* all came before the word, so I had to reread most of the paragraph. The *wretched conditions* are the dirt floor, no lock on the door, the horrible smell, and three flights of rickety stairs. *Wretched conditions* means a place unfit for people because it was unsanitary and unsafe."

4 Continue the process with the second sample.

5 Ask students to study the third sample. In their journals, students can jot down the clues they used.

6 Call for volunteers to share the clues they uncovered.

7 Repeat this demonstration several times. Continue to collaborate with students until you sense they are ready to work in groups or pairs.

Robb's Transparancy Examples for Fourth-Grade Mini-Lesson

The Kings wanted to share the daily struggles of the people they were trying to help. Their apartment was up three flights of rickety stairs. There was no lock on the front door and the lobby had a dirt floor. The barely heated building smelled horrible. Coretta was shocked by these *wretched conditions.*

> —From *Dare to Dream: Coretta Scott King and the Civil Rights Movement by Angela Shelf Medearis* (Lodestar), page 42.

Cricket spent the rest of her ride in the wheelchair and all of her lunchtime *speculating*. Who could be coming to visit her? She mentally ran down the names of all the girls in her class.

> —From *Spring Break* by Johanna Hurwitz (Morrow), page 40.

Terrified, Mongke *abandoned* his pouch and galloped away.
"More than a hero, I want a *prudent* husband who won't get himself killed at the first opportunity."

> —From *The Khan's Daughter* by Laurence Yep (Scholastic)

Steps to Organize Students for Using Vocabulary in Context

1. Encourage students to identify four to five difficult words. You can select words you feel students need to study, or you can share the selection with students. My advice is to vary the process, for it is important for students to identify words that stump them and observe how they can discover meanings within the text.

2. Divide the class into pairs and/or groups of four.

3. Reserve time for five to six students to share their processes each day.

4. Encourage students to apply these strategies while reading across the curriculum.

Eighth Graders Call on Context Clues

*T*o support their study of the Great Depression, eighth graders read Irene Hunt's *No Promises in the Wind*. I divided the book into five chunks. After reading each section, students raise questions for discussion, talk about how each part informs them about the Depression, and complete journal responses. In addition, five groups of four students work on using context clues to discover the meanings of four to five difficult words in each section.

One group has identified these words while reading the first sections: *rancor*, page 11; *improvident*, page 13; *paltry*, page 27. Students help one another explore clues in the text, then in their journals; they write the word and its meaning in their own words. What follows is a transcription of part of one group's conversation.

Adam: It says that the dad usually agreed with his wife before hard times.

Katie: But near the end of the paragraph it says that Dad became bitter about Josh's practicing the piano.

Nicole: If it was earlier *without rancor* and now he [Dad] is bitter, maybe *without rancor* means without being bitter about it.

Clarke: Reread the sentence and put in *without being bitter* for *without rancor* and see if it makes sense.

Together, these students pool their understanding of various strategies to discover the meaning of a word as the author used it. Working in pairs or small groups transforms this activity into a shared experience where students, like detectives, use clues to solve the mystery of a word's meaning.

Word Collections for Struggling Readers

Since a limited reading, speaking, and writing vocabulary is a characteristic of struggling readers, I want to cultivate a deep interest in words among these students. To achieve this, each student will need a small plastic box that holds 3-by-5-inch index cards, a set of alphabet dividers, and index cards. On each index card, students record one word that the class has studied as well as a word they've explored from their reading. On the back of the card, students use their own words to explain the word's meaning.

While you monitor, teach, and support struggling readers for 15 to 20 minutes several times a week, other students can read, work on a journal response, or discuss their books. Here are some suggestions for using these word boxes with pairs of students:

❊ **SORT WORDS BY MEANING:** Partners can search for words that have similar meanings and/or opposite meanings, say each word aloud, then discuss words with each other. Partners can also search for words in their boxes that can be added to each partner's list.

❊ **DISCUSS MEANINGS OF WORDS:** Partners can select four to five words from their collections and talk about meanings with each other.

❊ **SORT WORDS BY PART OF SPEECH:** To reinforce parts of speech being studied, ask pairs to find examples of verbs, nouns, adjectives, or adverbs.

❊ **WRITE SENTENCES:** Following discussions, pairs can help one another write sentences that show they understand how the word functions in our language.

❊ **USE WORDS DURING WRITING WORKSHOP:** Word collections become a terrific spelling resource when students draft or revise pieces. Encourage students to dip into their collections to find alternate verbs, nouns, and correct spellings while working independently and to help peers during revision and editing conferences.

Root of the Week Chart

Quite often—especially in math and science class—a root, such as *ology* or *numer*, is the focus of study for several classes. That is the ideal time to set up a Root of the Week Chart. Place a piece of large chart or construction paper on a wall. Each day spend a few minutes reviewing the meanings of the list of words based on the root and invite students to add words. Here is a list of words that seventh graders collected while studying transversals in geometry.

Root of the Week: *trans*, Latin—*across, over, change, versus*

- transversal
- transfer
- transcontinental
- transition
- transit
- transaction
- transcribe
- transatlantic
- transistor
- transform
- transformer
- transgress

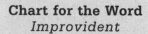

Chart for the Word *Improvident*

Part of Speech:
adjective

What Students Already Know:

- Someone who avoids work
- Someone who enjoys wasting time
- Someone who might get others to do the work
- A person who lounges around most of the time
- A person who is forever on vacation

Other Ways of Saying Improvident:

lazy
shiftless
timewaster
negligent
wasteful
careless

Situations:

- avoiding work
- not helping
- playing truant
- lazing around

Antonyms:

hardworking
diligent
careful
industrious
conscientious

Students' Sentences:

1. The prodigal son in the Bible was *improvident*.
2. The little red hen's friends were *improvident* because they never wanted to help her.
3. That *improvident* salesman never waited on any customers who came into the store.

Vocabulary Quilting

There will be times when almost everyone in your class pinpoints a difficult word or when students need a deeper understanding of a key word while studying a topic. The strategy that I call Vocabulary Quilting provides an in-depth study of a word. Like a quilt, you start with one square—the new word—and add squares (additional words) as you discuss synonyms, situations, sample sentences, and antonyms.

Set aside 15 to 20 minutes at least twice a week to introduce the word. Record the process on large chart paper, and hang the charts so students can reread them.

The steps that follow show how I linked what students already knew about the word *improvident*, a word that many eighth graders stumbled over during our study of *No Promises in the Wind*.

1. Think of a synonym students might have for the new word. I use *lazy* and ask students, "What happens if you're lazy at school or on a job?" After exchanging anecdotes, I introduce the word *improvident* and print it at the top of the chart.

2. Next, I print what students know about *improvident* under the heading "What Students Already Know." These are the ideas they've discussed after I posed the question about laziness on the job and at school.

3. Students skim page 13 in their books, pausing to read with care the sentence that contains *improvident*.

4. Students talk in groups, sharing what they understand about the word *improvident* and trying to think of synonyms or words with similar meanings. I write these under "Other Ways of Saying Improvident."

5. Then groups try to think of situations where they might use *improvident*. I write these on the chart under "Situations."

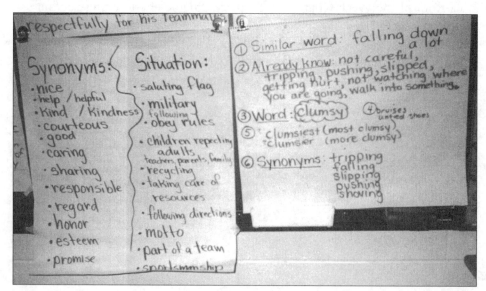

▲ *A vocabulary quilting chart created by fourth graders*

VOCABULARY CONNECTIONS   Abby & Jeremy

Similar Word suction-cling-pull

Word: Gravity

Part of Speech: Noun

What Students Already Know: Gravity is what pulls things to the center of the Earth. There is no gravity in space. Gravity keeps us from floating around the room.

Synonyms: Attraction - wheit - low - pitch- farality

Situations: We need gravity to keep us on the ground and also objects floating - hovering - flying - waitless

Antonyms: floating - hovering - flying - waitless

Sample Sentences: Gravity pulls us to Earth. If we did not have gravity we would bounce around the room.

VOCABULARY CONNECTIONS

Similar Word Surprised

Word: Stunned

Part of Speech - verb

What Students Already Know:
- I know that stunned means to be surprised and is something unexpected.
- Stunned is also to be scared.

Synonyms or Words With Similar Meanings: Synonyms for stunned would be to be scared, very surprised, and not knowing what is going to happen.

Situations: You might be stunned when you recieve a surprise birthday party

Antonyms or Words With Opposite Meanings: Some antonyms for stunned are to not be scared, and to be aware of what is going to happen.

Sample Sentences:
I was stunned when I went home and my dad jumped out from behind the door.

I was stunned when I received a surprise party from my parents.

▲ *Partners in fourth and fifth grade pool their knowledge to understand new words.*

6. On the chart, I model several ways that the word works in a sentence. You can also discuss its part of speech and print that on the chart.

7. On another day, students create original sentences that I add to the chart.

8. Sometimes I call for antonyms and record these on the chart.

9. Now that students have begun to expand their knowledge of the new word, you can ask them to uncover what information the dictionary offers.

10. Display the chart, and use the word frequently.

STANDARDIZED TEST LINK

T he Vocabulary Quilting strategy supports vocabulary tests in two ways:
1. It asks students to think of situations where they can use a new word. On a test, the situation surrounding an unfamiliar word often provides clues for understanding its meaning. 2. Students explore synoymns and antonyms, which expands their knowledge of a word.

Vocabulary Quilting

Word:

Part of Speech:

What Students Already Know:

Synonyms:

Situations:

Antonyms:

Sample Sentences:

Recreate the form at left and photocopy it for students. Invite them to work in pairs or small groups to fill out the forms after you've worked collaboratively with them.

Closing Reflections

I have become quite conscientious about reserving time, perhaps several classes each week, for vocabulary building. Even proficient readers who have rich personal reading lives enjoy exploring the origins and varied meanings of words.

Avoid testing your students. Vocabulary tests send the message that we should memorize words to pass exams rather than deepen our understanding of their meaning. Instead, listen to your students talk and carefully read their writing to see whether they successfully incorporate some new words. Help your students recognize that words enable them to think deeply about their world, imagine and pretend, and communicate with others through talk and writing. When you provide students with such clear and meaningful purposes, they will approach vocabulary building with thought and energy.

After-Reading Vocabulary Activities

> **"**If I use new words a lot, I can remember them.**"**
>
> —*Sixth Grader*

> **"**I knew it [the word] two weeks ago, but I haven't used it since then.**"**
>
> —*Seventh Grader*

> **"**We studied those words in October, how can I be expected to remember them in April?**"**
>
> —*Eighth Grader*

Student comments like these reveal so much about the difference between being introduced and quizzed on a new word and forming a lasting relationship with that word. No doubt, all of us hope our students will complete the school year with an abundance of newly learned words they will use as they read, write, think, and speak.

Activities in this chapter can boost students' recall of new words by providing them with multiple opportunities to use a word after the reading or unit has been completed. Once students integrate new words into their prior knowledge and experience, information moves from short-term to long-term memory.

Fourth graders share their descriptions of characters at the beginning and end of a story.

Build a Bank of Character Descriptors

Early in the school year when I ask students to describe a character's personality, they usually offer general words such as *nice*, *pretty*, or *kind*, or they describe the character's physical appearance. Students offer these general words because they usually have not engaged in thoughtful reflection about a character. To collect specific words that pinpoint a character's personality requires that students locate, think, and talk about these parts of a story:

- ☀ dialogue

- ☀ setting

- ☀ conflicts

- ☀ character's interactions

- ☀ character's inner thoughts

- ☀ character's motivations and decisions

The search for detailed descriptive words enlarges students' vocabulary and enables them to draw more meaningful conclusions about characters.

Fourth grade teacher Heather Campbell reviews a character description chart with students.

MINI-LESSON

Build a Word Bank of Character Descriptors

PURPOSE

to help kids describe characters from books using more precise, accurate words

MATERIALS

chart paper, marker pens, books students are reading

SUGGESTIONS FOR PRESENTING YOUR DEMONSTRATION:

1 Record on chart paper a general word that students use to describe a character. Fifth graders describe Sam Gribly in Jean Craighead George's *My Side of the Mountain* as *smart, resourceful, capable, clear thinking*.

2 Invite students to offer descriptive words. Fifth graders add *risk taker, adventurous, inventive,* and *skillful* to the list.

Tips for Organizing Students

1 Ask students for adjectives and nouns that describe a favorite character in a book they are reading. Write their words on chart paper. Sixth graders typically offer words such as *mean, troublemaker, nice, cool, a pain,* and *scared*.

2 Organize the class into pairs or groups of three to four.

3 Ask each pair or group to think of adjectives and nouns that have the same meanings as the words on the chart, but are more specific. Sixth graders offered these alternates for *mean: deceitful, sneaky, a liar, controlling,* and *vicious*.

4 Allow students to use the dictionary. Caution them to include synonyms they understand.

TIP BOX

Advertise Words That Describe Characters

Since a list of words that pinpoint characters' personalities can support struggling and proficient readers all year long, you'll want to continue to collect words throughout the year.

Once students have learned to use specific words to draw conclusions about a character's personality, give them a copy of this list to keep in their response journals. Adapt the list for fourth and fifth graders. Students should understand the words on the list so they can use them independently.

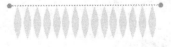

5 As a whole class, discuss the words groups came up with. List students' suggestions on a chart, under the appropriate words. Post the chart so students can refer to it during book talks.

6 To take this activity one step further, have partners and groups sort the words into various categories: adjectives and nouns, positive and negative traits, and traits that describe a character from a recently completed book.

STRATEGY IN ACTION

Sixth Graders Seek Words That Describe Characters

Sixth graders Patrick, Christian, and Tommy had been reading and discussing a collection of short stories by Avi, *What Do Fish Have to Do With Anything?: And Other Stories.* I asked each student to pick a character and search for words that describe his or her personality. *Cool, nice,* and *quiet* were words that all three boys offered. I asked the boys questions such as: What about your character made you say he or she was *cool, nice,* or *quiet*? What did he or she do? Say? Think? Then I have them skim and reread parts of the story, think about each passage they've reread, and search for accurate words that describe a character.

To give the boys a jump start, I suggested a word for each of the three and printed the words on the chart (see below). During three consecutive reading periods, I reserved 15 minutes and invited students to discover specific words for the general headings.

Words That Describe Characters' Personalities

NICE	QUIET	COOL
considerate	worried	popular
supportive	secretive	talkative
sympathetic	loner	courageous
concerned	shy	vivacious
helpful	introvert	heroic
generous	fearful	artistic
thoughtful	cautious	musical
kind		daredevil

Students used the specific words to discuss their characters. The criteria for discussion was to have an example from the story that supported the *selected word.* When you set aside time for thinking and discussion, you'll find that students can generate more specific descriptive words. Rich and meaningful talk helps students clarify their understanding.

Sample Word Wall of Adjectives
That Describe a Character's Personality

adaptable	dependent	imaginative	realistic
adventurous	determined	impatient	reasonable
affected	dignified	incompetent	rebellious
affectionate	discreet	inhibited	reckless
aggressive	distrustful	indignant	reflective
assertive	docile	insightful	relentless
aloof	dominant	insincere	sarcastic
anxious	dauntless	intelligent	secretive
arrogant	doubting	innocent	self-centered
autocratic	dynamic	inventive	sentimental
bitter	egotistical	irresponsible	self-controlled
boastful	evil	irresistible	skillful
bossy	enterprising	knowledgeable	show-off
brutal	empathetic	loyal	snobbish
callous	excitable	loving	sophisticated
capable	fickle	lazy	spiteful
careless	foolish	listener	spineless
candid	foolhardy	liar	stubborn
cautious	foresighted	methodical	spontaneous
charitable	frail	malignant	tyrannical
charming	friendly	modest	timid
clear thinking	gracious	moral	teasing
clever	gullible	moody	trustworthy
coarse	hardheaded	morbid	taker
cold	harsh	meticulous	treacherous
confident	heroic	oblivious	tormentor
cruel	hostile	overbearing	tolerant
confused	helpful	optimistic	unscrupulous
congenial	hateful	nonchalant	unconcerned
conscientious	hopeful	ornery	uncouth
conceited	happy	peculiar	uncompromising
cool	haughty	pessimistic	ungrateful
cooperative	honest	persevering	unhappy
courageous	hysterical	passive	unpopular
cowardly	humane	poised	uncooperative
cruel	humble	practical	unique
cynical	humorous	prudent	vulgar
daring	idealistic	planner	witty
dependable	impulsive	peacemaker	weak

Response Journals: Thinking on Paper

Following up a discussion of character traits with response journals or other written work not only helps students clarify their understanding of words, but also asks them to take the next step and think on paper. Equally as important, written work provides you with an assessment tool that can quickly identify students who understand a strategy well enough to move from talk to writing and those who need additional help from you.

Fourth graders find examples to support words that describe Ann Hamilton from The Cabin Faced West.

An eighth grader finds support for words that describe Aunt Alexandra from To Kill a Mockingbird.

Two Response Journal Strategies

Prove It Chart

PURPOSE

to collect examples from a story that support students
conclusions about characters personality traits

MATERIALS

chart paper, marker pens, students response journals, book or story
students are reading

SUGGESTIONS FOR PRESENTING
YOUR DEMONSTRATION:

1 Write you name and the date at the top of the chart.

2 Print the title of the story or book and the author under your name. With fourth graders, I use *Jonkonnu: A Story From the Sketchbook of Winslow Homer* by Amy Littlesugar.

3 Divide your paper in half, lengthwise. Students can fold their journal pages in half.

4 On the left-hand side, write the character's name and underneath it, "Personality Traits." I choose Cilla, the young white girl who watches Mr. Homer paint free, but segregated, African Americans. For personality traits, I note *curious* and *independent thinker*.

5 On the right-hand side, write "Example from the Story." For *curious*, I write: *Cilla follows Mr. Homer many times and hides to watch him paint and listen to the talk.*

6 Have students select a word from the class chart that describes another character from *Jonkonnu*. Write the word on the chart. Students offer *uncompromising* for Winslow Homer.

7 Have students briefly retell an example from the story that supports the trait. For support, students retold the part when Mr. Homer stares down the white man who threatens him for painting the African Americans. One student added that Homer ignores the gossip of the "white folk" and returns to the African American community.

8 Have students select another trait, discuss it, then offer an example from the story for you to record on the chart.

Tips for Organizing Students

1 Organize students into pairs.

2 Ask students to select a book they recently completed, and have students set up their journals, choose a character, and write two to three traits.

3 Invite students to complete a similar entry in their journals and share it with one another.

4 As students gain experience and demonstrate they can successfully complete such an entry, you can invite them to find support for several traits.

NAME: Cody S.   DATE: March 11, 1998

TITLE: Harold and the   AUTHOR: Donald Carrick
        Giant Knight.

BEGINNING   ENDING

WRITE CHARACTER'S NAME   SAME NAME
Harold   Harold

1. TRAIT Helpful   1. TRAIT planner

2. TRAIT hopeful   2. TRAIT daring

helpful PROOF Harold was because he helped on the farm when the Knights were there.

PROOF Harold was a good planner because he made the monster out of a basket to scare the knights away.

◀ *A fourth grader reflects on a character's traits and actions at the beginning of a story and at its end.*

A Character From Beginning to End

1 to 3 are the same as in the Prove It Chart mini-lesson.

4 On the left-hand side, write "Personality at the Beginning." Halfway down the left-hand side, write "Proof." For a survival study, seventh graders have just completed *Walkabout* by James Vance Marshall. To model this journal entry, I choose Mary and Peter.

5 On the right-hand side, write "Personality Traits at End." Halfway down the same side, write "Proof."

6 Select three words from the chart that describe your character at the beginning of the book or story. I write: *Mary and Peter were frightened, insecure, and dependent on each other and the Aborigine.*

7 Find a story example to support each trait. Here are the examples I offer: *Mary and Peter, her brother, are alone in the Australian Outback. Their plane has crashed; the pilot is dead. They have no food, water, clothing, shelter, radio, or compass.*

8 and 9 Repeat steps 6 and 7, finding traits that illustrate changes in the character. At the end, I note, the children are confident, self-sufficient, and hopeful. After the Aborigine died, the children learned to find food, water, and communicate with other Aborigines—they are adults, not children. They know they will find the white people's house and return home.

This entry is a terrific way to point out that characters change as they live through experiences. For a follow-up discussion, invite students to talk about the events, other characters, and decisions that caused these changes. You'll find that such discussions offer opportunities to think with specific words as well as enlarge students' knowledge of why characters change.

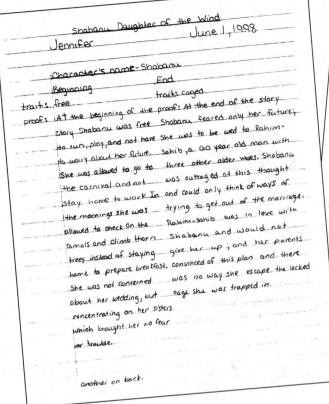

An eighth grader considers the changes in the character Shabana that occurred in the course of the novel.

Word Activities and Games

After students have discussed and thought about new words, invite them to play games and/or complete thought-provoking activities independently or with a partner. You will not always have the time to formally include additional games and activities. That's okay.

Analogies Test Concept Connections

I ask my eighth graders, "What strategies do you use to figure out the analogy questions that make up the verbal aptitude section of the Comprehensive Testing Program (CTP) our school administers each spring?" Here are some of these responses:

- I guess.

- I have no strategies. I hope for the best.

- Some I just know—others, forget it.

- I study the first pair and try to make the second pair like it.

The last student was close, but most students had no idea that they could develop helpful, analytical strategies. Since analogies are part of many standardized tests, it's important to understand how these comparisons work.

How Analogy Problems Appear on Tests

Create practice tests for students with analogies using all of the ways tests format these questions:

1. panic is to terror as reveal is to

   (a) mask   (b) remake   (c) disclose   (d) cover

2. grieve:rejoice :: realistic: (The single colon stands for "is to"; the double colon stand for "as." Students read the question this way: grieve is to rejoice as realistic is to_____.)

   (a) thinking   (b) artistic   (c) imaginary   (d) accurate

3. beak:buzzard :: (Students read the analogy this way: beak is to buzzard as _____ is to _____.)

   (a) nose: nostril   (b) tusk: boar   (c) kangaroo : pouch   (d) soar: eagle

All Kinds of Analogies

Here are some examples of the kinds of relationships analogies present. An excellent resource for you and students are the series of practice books, titled *Analogies: Concept Questions, Levels A–F*, Continental Press, 520 East Bainbridge St., Elizabethtown, PA 17022; (800) 233-0759. Examples that follow are from Level F.

*In the kinds of analogies that follow, word order is **not** important.*

Synonyms
Example:
surge:rise :: renew: (a) alive (b) restore (c) dead (d) drain

Antonyms
Example:
vicious is to kind as reckless is to (a) careful (b) risk (c) unsafe (d) healthy

Rhyming Words
Example:
Thatch:catch :: loud: (a) quiet (b) crowd (c) cloudy (d) noise

Homophones
Example:
gilt:guilt :: (a) read:read (b) jump:jumped (c) core:corps (d) bruise:bruises

Fun Portmanteau Words to Share

autobus
automobile + bus

bit
binary + digit

because
by + cause

chortle
chuckle + snort

clash
clap + crash

con man
confidence + man

STANDARDIZED TEST LINK

"Now that I try to figure out the relationship in the sample analogy, my practice test scores have soared," said Douglas, an eighth grader. Teaching students how to deal with analogy questions, then providing lots of practice, is the best way to improve test-taking skills. Replacing wild guesses with a thoughtful, critical approach to figuring out the relationship makes all the difference in students' success levels.

Parts of the Same Thing

Example:

lens:frame :: (a) dominoes:checkers (b) propeller:wing (c) miner:gold (d) fraction:number

Two Examples From the Same Class

Example:

meteor:comet :: dolphin: (a) porpoise (b) net (c) ocean (d) boat

In the kinds of analogies that follow, word order is important. The answer students select should be in the same order as the example.

Different Forms of the Same Word

Example:

describe is to description as organize is to (a) organizing (b) organization (c) organizer (d) organ

Name and Location

Example:

state:Ohio :: city: (a) Michigan (b) Cleveland (c) town (d) river

A Class and an Example of That Class

Example:

female:ewe :: (a) cattle:herd (b) grease:slimy (c) hockey:soccer (d) musician:harpist

Item and Who Uses It

Example:

car is to motorist as church: (a) icon (b) priest (c) stained glass (d) cross

Item and What It Does

Example:

scissors:cut :: (a) ruler:straight (b) operator:telephone (c) orbit:spacecraft
(d) microscope:magnify

Name and Descriptor

Example:

pocketknife:sharp :: ravine: (a) rock (b) dangerous (c) river (d) narrow

Whole and a Part

Example:

woodpile:log :: (a) tablecloth:stain (b) baggage:suitcase (c) lumber:barge
(d) collection:assemble

Action and Where It Takes Place

Example:

deposit is to bank as flood is to (a) river (b) evacuate (c) water (d) waves

Action and Who Does It

Example:

applaud:audience :: (a) thief:steal (b) perform:singer (c) happy:sad
(d) racehorse:gallop

Sequence

Example:

spring:summer :: (a) morning:early (b) time:hour (c) month:June
(d) morning:afternoon

Degree

Example:

acquaintance:friend :: (a) genuine:real (b) enemy:fight
(c) introduce:introduction (d) crevice:ravine

Teaching Analogies

PURPOSE

to show students the types of relationships they'll meet in analogies

MATERIALS

sample analogies, chart paper, marker pens

SUGGESTIONS FOR PRESENTING YOUR DEMONSTRATIONS:

1 On large chart paper, write this sample analogy:

circle:circumference :: rectangle:
(a) perimeter   (b) ratio   (c) angle   (d) area

2 Show students how to read it and review the meanings of the single and double colons (see page 75).

3 Think aloud, modeling how you discover the relationships between the words.

4 Here is what I told students:
The *circumference* is the outer edge or rim of the circle. I need to find an answer that gives the outer edge of a rectangle. *Area* is the amount of space inside the rectangle, *ratio* is a relationship, *angle* is one of the four right angles, so *perimeter* is the best answer, because it is the distance around the outside of a rectangle.

5 Organize students into groups of three to five. Give each group an analogy written on an index card. Challenge the group to decide the correct answer and explain, in detail, why they selected it rather than the other choices.

6 Continue to present different kinds of analogies and set aside class time for students to practice.

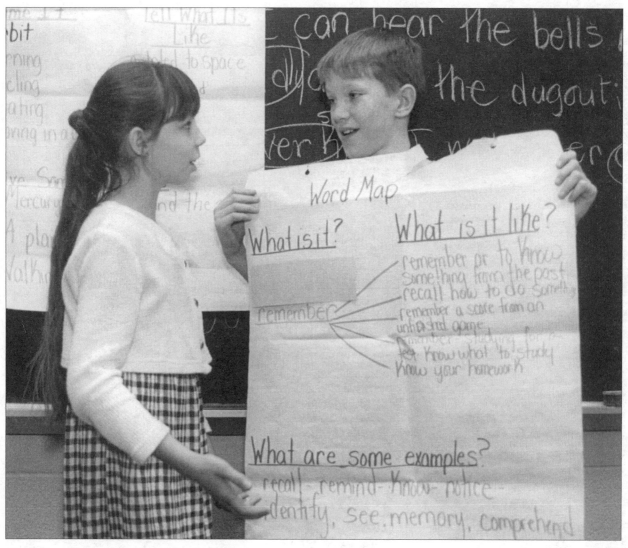

▲ *Fourth graders share their word map with classmates.*

Mapping a Word

This is a top-notch method of reviewing a topic students have studied, such as *whales*; a concept, such as *revolution*; or a key word, such as *orbit*. This activity works best when pairs or groups of three to four students collaborate on the map, making responses richer and varied.

Have students share their maps with classmates and encourage them to ask one another questions. I've included a map composed by a group of fourth graders who researched sharks. These maps also become evidence of the learning that has taken place.

Shark Group's Review

MAPPING A WORD

NAME IT
Shark

TELL WHAT IT'S LIKE
• cold blooded
• sharks adapt to water temperature
• many have rows of teeth, up to 20 rows
• swallows prey in parts or whole- doesn't chew, just tears
• skin has little teeth: denticles
• some travel great distances
• has 6 senses: hearing, smell, sight, 2 kinds of touch-distant & close, electro reception - tiny pores called ampullae pick up electric signals other animals give off.
• reproduce like mammals as eggs fertilized inside females
• shark pups hatch in 6-15 months
• size varies: size of hand to size of a school bus

GIVE SOME EXAMPLES
whale sharks, nurse sharks, sand tiger sharks, mako, white, horn sharks, cat sharks, hammer head, dwarf sharks

Two word maps done by fourth graders.

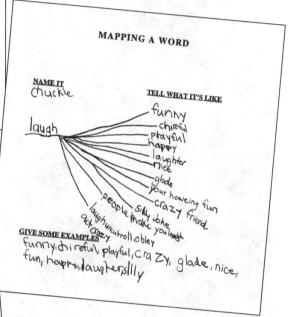

MAPPING A WORD

NAME IT
chuckle

laugh

TELL WHAT IT'S LIKE
funny
chireful
playful
happy
laughter
nice
glade
your howeing fun
crazy friend
silly joke
people make you laugh
laugh uncutroll obley
act crazy

GIVE SOME EXAMPLES
funny, chireful, playful, crazy, glade, nice, fun, happy, laughterslly

Word Map

What is it?
deteriorating

What is it like?
disintegrating
rotting (like a p...
perishing (stinki...
getting black + bl...
going away
becoming junk
collapsing (falling...
Ramshackled

Becoming worse

Fifth grade word map.

Mapping a Word

Name It

Tell What It s Like

Give Some Examples

Recreate this form to use with your students. ▶

Math Concept Web

Webbing in math class can broaden students' understanding of number and develop a rich mathematical vocabulary. Create the web with mathematical symbols and numerals. Start the web on construction or chart paper, and set aside a few minutes each day to add items.

After students complete the web, ask them to translate symbols into words and record these words on chart paper. Here are the words fifth graders offered:

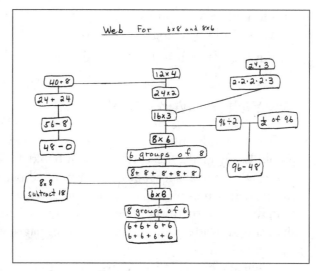

▲ *A fifth grade's web for 8 X 6*

forty	plus	addends	sum
eight	groups	five	one
minus	difference	remainder	subtract
multiples	multiply	subtraction	multiplication
groups	product	minuend	subtrahend
multiplier	multiplicand	seven	twenty-four
three	fifty-six	times	thirty-two
sixteen	division	divided by	quotient
two	four	commutative	fraction
primes	exponents	composites	factors

Extend Students' Word Knowledge

With these activities that use the charted words, you can deepen students' knowledge and understanding of math vocabulary.

Have students write each word on a small index card that's been cut in half. Store words in sealable plastic bags so they can be used again.

Student Activities

Besides sorting, have students explain the reasons behind the ways they organized words.

1. Organize or sort words acccording to mathematical operation.

2. Find pairs of words that are similar and/or opposite in meaning.

3. Find words with prefixes. Use your knowledge of the prefix to explain each word's meaning.

4. Find words with suffixes. Explain the part of speech each suffix implies.

My Writer s Word Book

To hook kids onto collecting words, I provide them with a writer's word book. Easily made, these 4-by-6-inch booklets consist of a colored-paper cover with several sheets of lined or unlined paper inside. Have students print their names on and decorate the cover. Students keep the notebooks handy—in their writing folders or response journals. While reading and listening to read-alouds, students can fill pages with words and phrases that intrigue them.

I tell students that I jot down words that catch my attention. Reading lists of words I've collected is like filling my creativity tank with high-test ideas. Often, I'll discover a word or phrase to use in a lead or to fine-tune a verb.

During workshop, encourage students to search for strong verbs or specific nouns in their word books. Sometimes, students who say "I have nothing to write about" will get an idea while reading a list of words that connect them to an event or memory.

Introduce and require that students try this strategy for several weeks. Not everyone is a word collector, but before abandoning a strategy, it's important to try it. After several weeks, I make writer's word books optional.

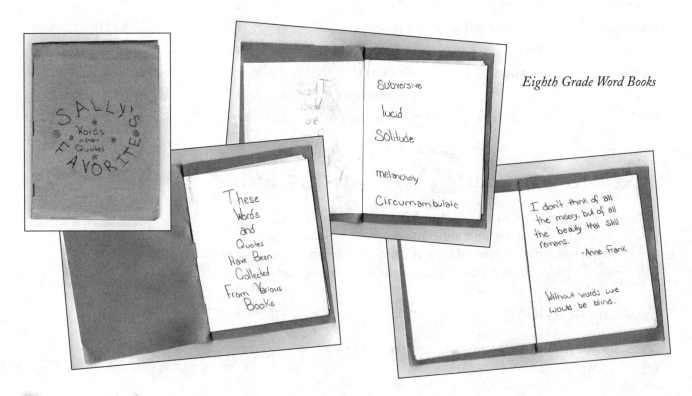

Eighth Grade Word Books

Vocabulary Concentration

In this spin-off of the game Concentration, students use their memories to match pairs of homophones, homographs, synonyms, or antonyms. Besides developing recall of word placement, students have to explain each matched pair in order to keep the cards they've matched.

Materials: a set of 16 to 20 or 24 cards with pairs of homophones, homographs, antonymns, or synonoyms (See pages 84-85.)

Players: two

Cards: Use 3 x 5 index cards to create different decks

Words: students should know the meanings of and be able to pronounce each word

Object: to find as many matched pairs as possible

Score: one point for each pair

How to Play:

1. First, thoroughly mix up cards.

2. One player arranges a deck of 16 cards, so words are face-down, into 4 rows of 4; arrange a deck of 20 cards into 4 rows of 5. The second player goes first.

3. The first player turns over two cards, looks at and replaces them in the same place. Players can see cards that each turns over.

4. Second player turns over 2 cards, looks at each and replaces them.

5. Players continue turning over pairs of cards trying to find matched pairs. The goal is to remember where cards are so a player can deliberately select a pair of matching cards.

6. Each player must correctly pronounce the words in a match and explain their meanings. If a player can't explain both words' meanings, then he puts the cards back in different parts of the deck.

7. The player with the most matched pairs wins.

Match-It Card Game

Create standard decks of 52 cards that contain 26 pairs of homophones, synonyms, or antonyms. Use this game to review words recently studied and for cumulative review of words.

Materials: a deck of 52 cards

Players: 2 to 4

Cards: Use 3 x 5 index cards to create a deck

Words: students should know the meanings of and be able to pronounce each word

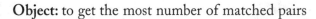

Object: to get the most number of matched pairs

Score: 1 point for each pair

How to Play:

1. One student mixes the deck of cards and gives them out.

2. Students take turns starting with the child to the left of the dealer.

3. Players receive 8 cards each and check hands for matching pairs.

4. If a player discovers a match, she says each word and explains their meanings. You can make the game more challenging by having players also use the word in a thoughtful sentence. When students can't explain the meanings of both words, they place the cards back in different parts of the deck.

5. Place remaining cards, words down, in the center of the playing area.

6. If players have matched pairs, they draw enough cards to have 8 in their hand.

7. First player draws a card, checks hand for matches, and places discarded card, faceup, next to the center pile.

8. A player can choose a discarded card to make a match.

9. Continue playing until all of the cards have been drawn from the word-down pile.

* Younger students might have trouble holding 8 cards in a fan shape. Each time they draw a card, students can check their stack one by one.

Sample sets of words

Each set has 26 words so it can be used for Concentration or Match It.

Easy Homophones	Challenging Homophones
prays, praise	rude, rued
sea, see	rye, wry
real, reel	trussed, trust
bold, bowled	vale, veil
stare, stair	insight, incite
billed, build	hostel, hostile
told, tolled	carat, caret
coarse, course	bouillon, bullion
ant, aunt	aural, oral
beach, beech	ascent, assent
foul, fowl	faint, feint
threw, through	profit, prophet
stake, steak	reek, wreak

Easy Homographs
lead, lead
read, read
record, record
contract, contract
conduct, conduct
sewer, sewer
sow, sow
dove, dove
tear, tear
object, object
wound, wound
content, content
close, close

Challenging Homographs
refuse, refuse
affect, affect
console, console
entrance, entrance
intern, intern
minute, minute
peaked, peaked
invalid, invalid
slaver, slaver
bass, bass
buffet, buffet
commune, commune
compact, compact

Synonyms
vacant, unoccupied
fetch, retrieve
grateful, appreciative
glum, morose
hide, conceal
honor, revere
regretful, penitent
unify, consolidate
fluctuate, vacillate
melt, dissolve
raid, invade
peak, summit
verify, substantiate

Antonyms
absent, present
loose, tight
panic, calm
permanent, unstable
aid, hinder
generous, stingy
ordinary, unique
transparent, opaque
wreck, create
revenge, forgiveness
segregate, integrate
blunt, sharp
maintain, discontinue

When Students Teach

Author and scientist Seymour Simon told me, "The best way to understand something is to have to teach it." When teachers apply Simon's keen observation to their classes, it's logical to invite students to teach, because the time invested in preparing for teaching deepens one's knowledge of a subject.

Fourth Graders Teach One Another About Fascinating Words

During reading workshop, fourth-grade teacher Heather Campbell invites her students into the world of words. Fourth graders mirror Heather's enthusiam for words and all of them write lists of words and phrases from their reading in small word log books.

On the morning I observe Heather's class, she explains that there are four groups, each reading different titles, and Christine, who is reading independently. One of Heather's goals is to introduce activities that invite students to return to their books. On a piece of large chart paper with the title and author written at the top, Heather asks students to skim their books and find three to four words that intrigued them—words that aroused their curiosity. Each group color-codes their lists, for students record selections on the chart with different color markers. To help her students prepare for their roles as teachers of words, Heather develops the criteria that follows with them:

- Reread the passage that contained the word. Think of the clues you used to determine its meaning. Share these with classmates.

- Look up your words in the dictionary and try to learn more about them.

- Tell why you chose each word.

Heather listens to each child's presentation and wraps up each one with positive feedback such as: "You really remembered each situation in your book that contained your words," or "Now I understand the meanings so clearly." If a child's explanation is incomplete or there are misspellings on the chart, Heather speaks to that student later, helping her make adjustments. "These kids can't wait to work on words," she tells me. "I want to take advantage of their joy in language—that's why we work on corrections privately."

Here are some words students selected, along with their comments:

mortal: *sounds neat—it's a human being like us—and can die.*
skee daddle: *funny sounding word—a weird way to say go away.*
toothy-smile: *that's a neat way to say a smile that shows all your teeth.*
(Brandon demonstrates one.)
jeering: *sounds mean—it's when you make fun of someone—you mock them.*

STRATEGY IN ACTION

Sixth-Grade Math Students Teach One Another

Once you discover that students have some knowledge and experience with a topic such as geometry, the Civil War, recycling, or pets, you can organize them into groups of four and then ask them to explore, study, and teach part of a topic to their classmates. To help students journey deeply into a topic, it's beneficial to provide them with criteria that you design with their input. That's just what Powhatan school's math teacher, Harry Holloway, did with his sixth graders. Harry invited students to review and learn more about the geometry chapter in their textbook. Their goal? To learn concepts and vocabulary well enough to effectively teach classmates.

As students read through the chapter, Harry set aside 15 minutes of each class for a week. During that time, he collaborated with students and created these guidelines:

1. Each group of four students will draw one of these topics, written on paper, from a box: *triangles, circles, polygons, quadrilaterals.*
2. Groups will plan and set up a large bulletin board in the library that contained these basic elements: a list of key vocabulary defined in their own words; constructions; models; illustrations.

Continued

Math 6 geometry project
Be as complete as possible.
Name Dillon
1) What group were you in?
Quadrilaterals
2) What did you do in your group?
I found information on quadrilaterals and I am going to talk for the presentation.

3) What did you learn? About your topic? What did you learn about the other topics? I learned that you can find quadrilaterals every where. I also learned that there are millions of quadrilaterals such as Golden rectangle, trapizoid, square, etc. I also learned from other topics that there are millions of polygons in a Nintendo 64 game.

4) What did you like about this project? Was this an effective way to study geometry? Explain Yes, I liked this project because you are allowed to work in groups. Yes, It was an effective way to study because you are allowed to get on the world wide web and use books and have fun at the same time.

5) What improvements would you suggest? Give the students a longer time to work. Wait to grade it after everyone is finished and find out what erased our definitions on the computer.

Math 6 geometry project
Be as complete as possible.
Name Smoot
1) What group were you in?
Polygons
2) What did you do in your group?
Built a board about polygons, I worked mostly on the internet, and word processing.

3) What did you learn? About your topic? What did you learn about the other topics?
I learned what polygons are, where they are used, how to work in a group, and types of polygons.

I learned what kind of circles, quadrilaterals, and triangles there are in the world. I liked watching other groups work.

4) What did you like about this project? Was this an effective way to study geometry? Explain
I LOVED working on this project with the kids in my group. It was so fun. It was much better than working in a book about fractions. It was much more effective than that.

Sixth graders' self-evaluation of teaching geometry project

3. Students will use the information on bulletin boards to teach material.
4. Students involve classmates in hands-on learning activities.
5. Groups will evaluate one another's bulletin boards.
6. Students will self-evaluate the project.

According to Harry, the project was a great success because students had studied some geometry in grades 4 and 5. "Presenting students with the goal of teaching others," Holloway pointed out, "gave students a focus and enabled them to understand the depth of learning needed to explain ideas with new vocabulary and develop meaningful activities for classmates."

Sixth graders' bulletin boards for polygons and triangles

Closing Reflections

*T*hink of the strategies in this book as a menu of activities to choose from. You won't use all of them each year. Select those you believe will move students forward and develop a lasting curiosity about words.

There will be times when a strategy doesn't work with a group of students. Often this occurs because students lack the background knowledge to connect to new words. When this happens to me, I rethink my demonstration and search for clues that will enable me to hook students. In addition to detective work, I always ask my students, "Why are you having difficulty with this activity?" or "Why didn't the mini-lesson work?" The sampling of student responses that follow illustrate how students' feedback can benefit instruction.

❋ "How can I understand <u>prime factors</u> and <u>factor trees</u> when I'm not sure what a <u>factor</u> is?" —*Grade 5*

❋ "If <u>habitat</u> is a home, then it's my address. But you keep looking for more [ideas]." —*Grade 4*

❋ "I can never think of the difference between <u>connotative</u> and <u>denotative</u>. The words don't stick in my head." —*Grade 7*

Words and background knowledge are the tools readers use to construct meanings from texts. Central to all reading development is vocabulary instruction that occurs before, during, and after studying a topic. Reserving time throughout the school year for word study can enlarge children's vocabulary and better equip them to deal with more difficult and complex texts.

Appendix

Greek and Latin Roots

Root	Origin	Meaning	Examples
act	Latin	do	action, transact
aero	Greek	air	aerobics, aerate
agri	Latin	field	agriculture, agrarian
alt	Latin	high	altitude, alto
alter	Latin	other	alternate, altercation
ambul	Latin	walk, go	ambulance, amble
amo, ami	Latin	love	amiable, amorous
ang	Latin	bend	angle, triangle
anim	Latin	life, spirit	animate, animal
ann, enn	Latin	year	annual, biennial
anthr	Greek	man	anthropology, misanthrope
apt, ept	Latin	suitable	apt, aptitude
aqua	Latin	water	aquaduct, aquarium
arch	Greek	chief	monarch, archenemy
arch	Greek	primitive,	ancient, archaic, archives
art	Latin	skill	artisan, artist
ast	Greek	star	astronaut, asterisk
aud	Latin	hear	audible, audition
baro	Greek	weight	barometer, isobar
belli	Latin	war	bellicose, rebellion
biblio	Greek	books	bibliography, Bible
bio	Greek	life	biology, biosphere
brev	Latin	short	abbreviate, brevity
cad, cas	Latin	fall, perish	cascade, cadaver
cal	Latin	hot	calorie, caldron
cam	Latin	field	campus, campaign
cand	Latin	glow, white	candle, candidate
cap	Latin	head	captain, decapitate
cardi	Greek	heart	cardiac, cardiogram
cede, ceed	Latin	go, yield	proceed, succeed
ceive, cept	Latin	take, receive	receive, accept
centr	Latin	center	central, eccentric
cert	Latin	sure	certain, certify
cess	Latin	go, yield	cessation, process
chron	Greek	time	chronic, chronicle
cide, cise	Latin	cut, kill	scissor, suicide
cip	Latin	take, receive	recipe, recipient
claim, clam	Latin	shout	clamor, exclaim
clar	Latin	clear	clarity, declare
cline	Latin	lean	decline, incline
clud	Latin	shut	conclude, seclude

Root	Origin	Meaning	Examples
cogn	Latin	know	incognito, recognize
commun	Latin	common	communal, commune
cord	Latin	heart	cordial, discord
corp	Latin	body	corpse, corporation
cosm	Greek	universe	cosmos, microcosm
crat	Greek	rule	autocrat, bureaucrat
cred	Latin	believe	credit, incredible
cur	Latin	care	cure, manicure
cur	Latin	run	current, recur
cycl	Greek	circle, ring	bicycle, cyclone
dem	Greek	people	democrat, epidemic
dic	Latin	speak	dictate, verdict
div	Latin	divide	divide, division
domin	Latin	master	dominate, dominion
don, donat	Latin	give	donate, pardon
duc	Latin	lead	conduct, educate
fac	Latin	make, do	benefactor, factory
fer	Latin	bear, carry	ferry, transfer
firm	Latin	securely fixed	affirm, confirm
flect	Latin	bend	deflect, reflect
form	Latin	shape	transform, uniform
frag	Latin	break	fragile, fragment
fug	Latin	flee	fugitive, refuge
funct	Latin	perform	function, malfunction
gen	Greek	birth, race	generate, progeny
geo	Greek	earth	geography, geology
gon	Greek	angle	diagonal, pentagon
grad	Latin	step, stage	grade, gradual,
gram	Greek	letter, written	grammar, telegram
graph	Greek	write	autograph, graph
grat	Latin	pleasing	gratify, ungrateful
greg	Latin	gather	aggregate, congregate
hab, hib	Latin	hold	habitat, prohibit
homo	Latin	man	homicide, hombre
hosp, host	Latin	host	hostess, hospital
hydr	Greek	water	hydrant, hydroelectric
iatr	Greek	medical care	geriatrics, podiatry
imag	Latin	likeness	image, imagery
init	Latin	beginning	initial, initiate
integ	Latin	whole	integer, integrate
junct	Latin	join	adjunct, juncture
jud, jur, jus	Latin	law	judge, justice, jury
lab	Latin	work	elaborate, labor
laps	Latin	slip	elapse, relapse
liber	Latin	free	liberate, liberty
loc	Latin	place	locate, location
log	Greek	word	dialogue, prologue
luc	Latin	light	lucid, translucent

Root	Origin	Meaning	Examples
lum	Latin	light	illumine, luminous
luna	Latin	moon	lunar, lunatic
man	Latin	hand	manual, manipulate
mand	Latin	order	command, mandate
mar	Latin	sea	mariner, submarine
mater, matr	Latin	mother	maternal, matron
mech	Greek	machine	mechanic, mechanize
mem	Latin	mindful of	memory, remember
ment	Latin	mind	demented, mental
meter	Greek	measure	diameter, centimeter
migr	Latin	change, move	migrate, migrant
miss	Latin	send	missile, missive
mit	Latin	send	admit, submit
mob	Latin	move	automobile, mobility
mon	Latin	advise	admonish, monitor
mort	Latin	death	mortal, mortician
mot, mov	Latin	move	promote, remove
narr	Latin	tell	narrate, narrative
nat	Latin	born	nation, native
nav	Latin	ship	naval, navigate
not	Latin	mark	denote, note
nun, noun	Latin	declare	announce, enunciate
nov	Latin	new	innovate, novel
numer	Latin	number	enumerate, numeral
ocu	Latin	eye	binocular, oculist
opt	Greek	eye	optic, optician
opt	Latin	best	optimal, optimist
ord	Latin	row	order, ordinal
orig	Latin	beginning	aborigine, origin
pater	Latin	father	paternal, patriarch
path	Greek	feeling, suffer	empathy, pathos
ped	Latin	foot	biped, pedal
pel	Latin	drive	compel, repel
pend	Latin	hang	appendix, suspend
phon	Latin	sound	telephone, phonics
photo	Greek	light	telephoto, photograph
phys	Greek	nature	physical, physician
poli	Greek	city	metropolis, police
pop	Latin	people	populace, popular
port	Latin	carry	import, porter
psych	Greek	mind	psyche, psychology
pug	Latin	fight	impugn, pugilist
put	Latin	think	deputy, computer
ques	Latin	ask, seek	inquest, question
rad	Latin	ray, spoke	radio, radius
rect	Latin	straight	erect, rectangle
reg	Latin	guide, rule	regal, regime
rid	Latin	laugh	deride, ridicule

Root	Origin	Meaning	Examples
rupt	Latin	break	erupt, rupture
sans	Latin	health	insanity, sanitary
scend	Latin	climb	ascend, transcend
sci	Latin	know	conscience, science
scop	Greek	see	microscope, periscope
scribe	Latin	write	inscribe, describe
script	Latin	wrote	transcript, script
sect	Latin	cut	dissect, intersect
sed	Latin	settle	sedate, sediment
sens	Latin	feel	sensation, senses
sent	Latin	feel	assent, consent
serv	Latin	save, keep	conserve, reserve
serv	Latin	serve	servant, service
sign	Latin	mark	insignia, signal
sim	Latin	like	similar, simile
sol	Latin	alone	desolate, solitary
solv	Latin	loosen	solvent, resolve
son	Latin	sound	sonar, sonnet
spec	Latin	see	inspect, spectator
spir	Latin	breath	inspire, perspire
sta	Latin	stand	stationary, stagnant
strict	Latin	draw right	constrict, restrict
struct	Latin	build	construct, instruct
sum	Latin	highest	summary, summit
tact	Latin	touch	contact, tactile
tang	Latin	touch	tangent, tangible
ten	Latin	hold	tenant, tenure
ten	Latin	stretch	tension, tendon
terr	Latin	land	terrrace, terrain
tex	Latin	weave	context, textile
the	Greek	god	monotheism, theology
therm	Greek	heat	thermal, thermos
tract	Latin	pull, drag	attract, tractor
trib	Latin	give	contribute, tribute
turb	Latin	confusion	disturb, perturb
urb	Latin	city	suburb, urban
vac	Latin	empty	evacuate, vacant
vag	Latin	wander	vagrant, vague
var	Latin	different	variety, vary
ven	Latin	come	advent, convene
ver	Latin	truth	verdict, veracity
vict	Latin	conquer	conviction, victor
vid	Latin	see	evidence, video
voc	Latin	voice	advocate, vocal
void	Latin	empty	avoid, devoid
vol	Latin	wish, will	benevolent, volition
volv	Latin	roll	involve, revolve
vor	Latin	eat	herbivorous, voracious

16 Intriguing EPONYMS: Words That Come From Names of People and Places

Word	Origin
America	Named for Amerigo Vespucci who worked for a company that outfitted ships for Columbus. He wrote stories about his own voyages and people today believe this Italian mapmaker explored North and South America.
bikini	Named for the Bikini Atoll in the Pacific Ocean, where the U.S. started testing atomic bombs. The two-piece, skimpy bathing suit shocked the audience at a fashion show in Paris, making people feel as if they'ed been hit by an atomic fashion bomb.
bologna	A city in northern Italy known for its smoked sausages.
Bunsen Burner	Named for Robert Bunsen, a German chemist who invented a small metal tube on a stand that burned a mixture of gas and air.
candy	Named for the young French Prince Charles de Conde (con-Day) who loved sweet, sugary treats.
cheddar	A white or yellow cheese invented in the village of Cheddar, England.
Ferris wheel	George Washington Ferris, an inventor and engineer, designed this ride for the 1893 World's Fair held in Chicago.
frankfurter	Though considered an American food, hot dogs or frankfurters came from Frankfurt, Germany.
Geiger Counter	The clicking instrument that detects sand measures radioactivity and cosmic rays was invented by the German physicist, Hans Geiger.

Word	Origin
hamburgers	These all-American meat patties were first cooked in Hamburg, Germany.
jeans	This strong cotton cloth was named for the Italian city of Genoa. Genoa in middle English, is spelled "Gene" or "Jean."
Levi's	Named for Levi Strauss, a German immigrant who during the California Gold Rush made heavy blue overalls with pockets reinforced with copper rivets.
marathon	A race named after the Greeks won the battle at Marathon in 490 B.C., a messenger ran 26 miles to bring the news to Athens.
sandwich	Named for the English Earl of Sandwich. While playing cards, the Earl told his servant to bring him roast beef wrapped in bread. Though hungry, he refused to leave the game, so he ate his "sandwich" while playing.
teddy bear	Predident Theodore "Teddy" Roosevelt loved to hunt. On a hunting trip, the president refused to shoot a small bear tied to a tree. In 1902, makers stuffed toy bears started calling these toy animals, "teddy bears" to honor the president.
thug	Thugs were a gang of professional hoodlums who roamed nothern India. The word comes from the Indain word "thag" which means cheat or thief.

Prefixes

Prefixes can be word parts added to the beginning of a root or base word (such as *dis*). Some prefixes can function as a complete word (such as *arch*). Use the list that follows as a resource for yourself and students.

a	not, without	hydro	water	poly	many
ab	away from	hyper	extra, beyond, over	post	after
ad	to, toward, against	hypo	under, below	pre	before
ante	before	il	not	pro	in favor of
anti	against, opposite	im	not	proto	earliest
arch	chief, senior	infra	below, underneath	pseudo	pretended
at	to, toward	inter	between	quadri	four
auto	self	intra	inside of	re	back, again
bi	two	ir	not	retro	backwards
be	about, become	iso	equal	self	of, over oneself
circum	around	mal	bad	semi	half
co	together	meta	altered, behind	sub	under, less than
con	with, together	micro	small	super	over, more than
contra	against	mini	small	supra	above, beyond
counter	against, in opposition	mis	wrongly, badly	tetra	four
de	down, away from	mono	single	trans	across, though
demi	half	multi	many	tri	three
dia	through, across	neo	new	ultra	beyond
dis	away, the reverse of, not	non	against, not	un	not, the reverse of
dys	bad	ob	in the way of	under	below, beneath
en	to cause, provide	octa	eight	uni	single, one
epi	to, against, added on	omni	all, general	up	up
ethno	race, nation	pan	whole	via	by way of
ex	out of, away from	para	alongside, similar	vice	in place of
extra	outside, beyond	per	through		
fore	previously, in front of	peri	around		

Suffixes

Suffixes are a combination of letters (such as *ancy*) or a single letter (such as *s*) added to the end of a base word. What follows is a sampling of common suffixes and the parts of speech they indicate.

NOUN SUFFIXES		SUFFIXES THAT FORM ADJECTIVES		SUFFIXES THAT FORM ADVERBS	SUFFIXES THAT CREATE A VERBAL FORM
age	hood	able	ical	ly	ate
al	ice	al	ish	wards	ed
ance	ism	er	ive	ways	en
ant	ist	est	less	wide	ing
ate	ment	ette, let	ous	wise	ise, ize, yze
ee	ness	ful	some		
ence	sion	fully	worthy		
ent	tain	ible			
er, or, ar	tion	ic			
ese	ure				
ess					

Bibliography

Barr, Rebecca, Marilyn Sadow, and Camille Blachowicz. *Reading Diagnosis for Teachers: An Instructional Approach*. New York: Longman, 1990.

Daniels, Anthony. *Analogies: Concept Connections, Level F*. Pennsylvania: The Continental Press, 1995.

Gillet, Jean Wallace and Charles Temple. *Understanding Reading Problems: Assessment and Instruction*, Third Edition. New York: HarperCollins, 1990.

Henderson, Edmund. *Teaching Spelling*. Boston: Houghton Mifflin, 1985.

Robb, Laura. *Easy-to-Manage Reading and Writing Conferences: Practical Ideas for Conferences That Work*. New York: Scholastic, 1997.

——— *Reading Strategies That Work: Teaching Your Students to Become Better Readers*. New York: Scholastic, 1996.

——— *Whole Language, Whole Learners: Creating a Literature-Centered Classroom*. New York: Morrow, 1994.

Children s Books Cited

Avi. *What Do Fish Have to Do With Anything?* Cambridge, MA: Candlewick Press, 1997.

Darling Kathy. *Chameleons on Location*. Photographs by Tara Darling. New York: Lothrop, Lee & Shepard, 1997.

Deary, Terry. *Horrible Histories: The Awesome Egyptians*. New York: Scholastic, 1996.

Fritz, Jean. *The Cabin Faced West*. New York: Puffin, 1987.

George, Jean Craighead. *The Moon of the Mountain Lions*. Illustrated by Ron Parker. New York: HarperCollins, 1991.

———*One Day in the Tropical Rain Forest*. Illustrated by Gary Allen, New York: HarperCollins, 1990.

——— *My Side of the Mountain*. New York: Dutton, 1959.

Henkes, Kevin. *Return to Sender*. New York: Puffin Books, 1997.

Hunt, Irene. *No Promises in the Wind*. New York: Grosset & Dunlap, 1970.

Hurwitz, Johanna. *Spring Break*. Illustrated by Karen Dugan. New York: Morrow, 1997.

Kehret, Peg. *Earthquake Terror*. New York: Cobblehill, 1996.

Lee, Harper. *To Kill a Mockingbird*. New York: Warner Books, 1982.

Littlesugar, Amy. *Jonkonnu: A Story From the Sketchbook of Winslow Homer*, illustrated by Ian Schoenherr. New York: Philomel, 1997.

Maestro, Betsy. *Coming to America: The Story of Immigration*. Illustrated by Susannah Ryan. New York: Scholastic, 1996.

Marshall, James Vance. *Walkabout*. Littleton, MA: Sundance, 1984.

McCullers, Carson. *"Sucker."* Junior Great Books Series 8, Volume 1. Chicago, Illinois: The Great Books Foundation, 1984.

Medearis, Angela Shelf. *Dare to Dream: Coretta Scott King and the Civil Rights Movement*. Illustrated by Anna Rich. New York: Lodestar, 1994.

Nix, Garth. *Sabriel*. New York: HarperCollins, 1995.

Paterson, Katherine. *The Great Gilly Hopkins*. New York: HarperCollins, 1978.

——— *Jacob Have I Loved*. New York: Thomas Crowell, 1980.

——— *The Master Puppeteer*. Illustrated by Haru Wells. New York: Avon Books, 1975.

Simon, Seymour. *Earthquakes*. New York: Morrow, 1991.

——— *Our Solar System*. New York: Morrow, 1992

Spinelli, Jerry. *The Library Card*. New York: Scholastic, 1997.

Stanley, Diane and Peter Vennema. *Cleopatra*. New York: Morrow, 1994.

Yep, Laurence. *The Khan's Daughter: A Mongolian Folktale*. Illustrated by Jean and Mou-Sien Tseng. New York: Scholastic, 1997.